REFLECTIONS ON

THE SHACK

REFLECTIONS ON

THE SHACK

*A Topical Discussion by Women
from Different Walks of Life*

Writers: Shae Cooke, Tammy Fitzgerald, Donna Scuderi, Angela Rickabaugh Shears

Cover designer, and page layout: Dominique Abney

DESTINY IMAGE® PUBLISHERS, INC.

P.O. Box 310, Shippensburg, PA 17257-0310

"Speaking to the Purposes of God for This Generation and for the Generations to Come."

This book and all other Destiny Image, Revival Press, MercyPlace, Fresh Bread, Destiny Image Fiction, and Treasure House books are available at Christian bookstores and distributors worldwide.

For a U.S. bookstore nearest you, call 1-800-722-6774.

For more information on foreign distributors, call 717-532-3040.

Or reach us on the Internet: www.destinyimage.com

ISBN 10: 0-7684-3127-1

ISBN 13: 978-0-7684-3127-8

For Worldwide Distribution, Printed in the U.S.A.

1 2 3 4 5 6 7 8 9 10 11 / 13 12 11 10 09

CONTENTS

PREFACE

Venturing this second time into The Powder Room brings a feeling of relief and anticipation. This time I know it will be clean and stocked with all the amenities and essentials, and that my three powder puff sidekicks will be there again with a refreshing flow of conversation, wit, and humor—real enough to touch today, spiritual enough to embrace tomorrow, and exciting enough to keep us reaching for our God-given destinies.

Come sit for awhile with us. The seats in front of the mirror are comfortable...and the lights just bright enough to reveal things you might like to know.

INTRODUCTION

As a *New York Times* and Amazon bestseller and endorsed by Christian *and* secular notables, *The Shack* has caused quite a stir in classrooms, board rooms, and blog rooms nationwide...and now in The Powder Room.

Millions have read *The Shack* and parts of it have touched hearts and minds in ways not before experienced. The initial tragedy stuns the moral senses, the bitterness jabs at the heart, the journey to forgiveness keeps us stumbling along, and reaching the destination brings joy and peace.

Along with some underlying controversial theological concerns, this book is ripe for some serious discussion—as well as some bantering and badgering.

As the four of us journey through *The Shack*, our views about life, loss, love, and God are as different as the shoes we wear and the lives we lead.

No doubt these wikipowderroom-type cliff notes about

The Shack will spark a fire within you to question your relationship with God, your family, your friends...and yourself.

1

Foreword, March?

Angela

◇◇◇◇◇◇◇◇◇◇

It's hard for me to understand why most readers (I'm told) rarely read the front matter (Epigraph, Foreword, Preface, Prologue, Intro) of books. The Foreword in *The Shack* is not to be skipped over because it provides an in-depth look into the main character's life and temperament, and his relationships, past, present, and foreshadowed future. The Foreword, written by Mack's friend, lays a solid foundation on which the remainder of the book rests.

I had to lol as I started reading the first chapter because instead of facing the torments of an ice storm, I was actually in the throes of a violent wind storm that blew down tree limbs across power lines, and our rural community was without electricity for 10 hours. Without a computer link from my home office to the outside world, I picked up *The Shack* and began reading...and laughing—until I read the part about the mysterious note from Papa about meeting him at the shack.

From the enjoyable descriptions of the scenery and humorous ice skating in the driveway scene to the ominous note and the references to his daughter Kate's state of mind, the tone changes quickly and I knew something was going to be revealed that was not good.

As a *Legally Blonde, Sleepless in Seattle,* and Philippians 4:8 kind of person, I'm not a hand-me-the-tissue-box *Titanic* or *Braveheart* fan.

Tammy

Angela, I agree—the Foreword is definitely *huge* in this one. An absolute must-read!

Then we have the first chapter. It drew me right in, I must say. Always a fan of slapstick, I enjoyed the magnificent wipe-out on the ice, especially with the vengeful tree looking on. Hey, I laugh because I sympathize.

Things look pretty normal on the surface in this chapter: Mack's chat with his wife and little routines are nothing special on the whole. Yet little hints crop up into view, popping out of their hiding places somewhere below the surface... hints that all is not right with this man's world. The note in the mailbox drags up some dark moments before Mack pushes them back down again.

In short, the first chapter's attraction is more than just some humorous narration. Whispers of "more than meets the eye" are weaving into this story already, making me oh so curious about what is really going on.

Shae
◇◇◇◇◇◇◇◇◇◇◇

Color me blonde (Nice 'n Easy #104). I knew I was picking up a fictional work but the Foreword and Chapter One read like non-fiction, so I was back and forth trying to figure it out. Real person *William* Paul Young authors the book while *Willie*, a fictional friend of the fictional main character writes the Foreword. Young and his editors describe the work as realistic fiction; true, but fictionalized in its account of the author's life.[1] Hmmm.

As a mother, and knowing the premise of the book, it was hard enough to pick up. The day I brought my newborn son, my first and only child home from the hospital, we received a telephone call from a man who didn't identify himself but seemed to know us. He asked about the baby by name, congratulated us, and then started to ask personal questions like, where is he now? Thinking it odd but not wanting to appear as though I didn't recognize his voice, I told him he was on his father's lap, that we were enjoying our first day together as a family after my long stay in the hospital. Suddenly, the man made sexual reference about what we could do to our precious infant—. We hung up and dialed 911 who traced the call to a telephone booth in a seedy part of the city. The pedophile had probably retrieved our names from the birth announcement in the paper and then looked up our listed telephone number. Of course that would mean he had our address too, and terror struck my heart. For weeks, months, I kept every window locked, terrified that he would try to hurt my baby. Everything for a while had a "dot, dot, dot" after it.

Thankfully *we* had warning. The use of ellipses in reference to this family's little one in chapter one suggests something terrible about to happen to her, in which there was no warning...

Endnote:

1. FAQ page accessed February 16, 2009, http://theshackbook .com/discuss/index.php?topic=1166.0.

Donna
◇◇◇◇◇◇◇◇◇◇◇◇

Thanks, Shae—I'm glad I'm not the only who grappled with the Foreword. I felt as though I'd slipped into the "looking-glass" and out again—a very "Sixties" experience in which I expected the White Rabbit, Grace Slick, and Timothy Leary to show up at any moment. ;)

The first chapter left me equally unsettled in a non-hallucinatory kind of way. The author threaded the needle of suspense and began to weave a sense of foreboding into the most mundane circumstances. It was clear that something was afoot; and it was bigger than an ice storm, a mailbox, and a married man left home alone.

It was for me, a cinematic experience in which the musical score drip...drip...drips on the back of your mind. There was a subtext of images buried in the narrative—the sense, for me, that Mack was being watched by an unspoken, unidentified presence whose motives were unknown and whose intent would soon be discovered. When Nan decided to stay the night at Arlene's, I wanted to coax her out of it, or at least plead with her to pray hard for Mack.

The mention of *"The Great Sadness,"* plus the juxtaposition of "underlying sadness" and an "unusually cheery" quality to Nan's voice, only adds to my apprehension about the backstory. Not being real comfortable with psychodramas or depictions of violence, I could easily be tempted to back out of *The Shack*.

But that would mean leaving the Powder Room. No dice.

Your Reflections

_____

_____

_____

_____

_____

_____

_____

_____

_____

_____

_____

_____

_____

_____

_____

_____

_____

_____

_____

_____

Foreword, March?

_____

_____

_____

_____

_____

_____

_____

_____

_____

_____

_____

_____

_____

_____

_____

_____

_____

REFLECTIONS ON *THE SHACK*

2

PHOTOS ON MILK CARTONS

Shae

The shack seems to be a metaphorical place of the heart that we fill with the things that are too difficult to think about or even ask, and where we meet with God One-on-one in the midst of those hard thoughts and questions. So the shack is a good place for you to be, Donna!

This chapter endeared and attached me to this precocious little girl, Missy, and magnified to me in a relatable way as a parent myself, the closeness of their father/daughter relationship. "Will God ever ask me to jump off a cliff," asked Missy after her daddy retold her and her sister Kate the redemptive analogy about the Indian maiden. Mack told her neither he nor God would ever ask something like that of her.

Mack's storytelling actually prepared me a tad better for the horrific details I know are to come. Getting to those details will be like a free-fall off a cliff of terror having had my son go missing once, for like all of three minutes and imagining the worst. Ours had a happy ending, but I can well understand why the author uses heavy words like draping, weighty, dulling, stooping, exhausting, bleak, despairing, murky, tightening, crushing, coiling, nausea, guilt, and regret in reference to The Great Sadness' emotional and physical effects.

Tammy

As we gear up to hear the story of Missy's disappearance, spending time beforehand to get a good look at the sweet, tender father/daughter relationship Mack and Missy have, I can only imagine how hard this will be to read, especially for parents. I'm already biting my lip for this poor family, knowing that something sinister is heading their way.

The sad legend of the Multnomah tribe's princess interrupts the happy family vacation with a taste of tragedy, certainly seeming to foreshadow the tragedy that waits for Mack and his family. At the same time, there is the slightest glimmer of hope—the princess saved her lover, and all the sick people in two tribes. Her sacrifice brought them redemption.

Perhaps, then, there will be redemption for Mack as well.

Angela

Who doesn't feel "the presence of God, out here surrounded by nature..." as Mack did on the family camping trip? When working in my flower beds, "playing in the dirt again," as my husband claims, I am as close to God as sitting in a padded pew or bowing my head in reverent prayer.

And asking questions: "Did it really happen?" and "So is Jesus dying a legend?" is as natural for children as falling off bikes and jumping on beds. When Missy asked her dad, she was searching for more than answers. Like we all do from time to time.

Like Missy's mom's prayers, the more we fill our children's and grandchildren's minds with God's Word, the more of a soft landing they have when hitting the pavement of disappointment or the floor of pain and suffering.

Second Timothy 1:5,7 comes to mind: When I call to remembrance the genuine faith that is in you, which dwelt first in your grandmother Lois and your mother Eunice, and I am persuaded is in you also. For God has not given us a spirit of fear, but of power and of love and of a sound mind.

Donna

Everything about Missy is precious. I imagine that, for parents, she brings to mind the close, sweet moments of a beloved child's growing-up years. For non-parents like me, it stirs my imagination about those kinds of experiences. When Mack draws Missy into his arms, I begin to imagine the warmth of their embrace, the smell of her hair, the sound of her breathing as she drops off to sleep.

And I try to imagine how devastating it would be to have your child—the one you held so close and comforted so often—disappear into thin air, or die in her youth.

Such tragedies happen every day. I just watched a news story about a five-year-old girl who recently vanished. We've seen the photos of missing children posted on milk cartons and billboards. We know terrible things happen to innocents, and it grieves us. But only the families who experience it firsthand can have a clue what it's really like.

Mack's unfolding story gave me a glimpse of *The Great Sadness*. As his heart breaks over Missy's poignant question in the dark, my heart breaks for them. No wonder Mack's arms "were sewn in...bleak folds of despair." No wonder he dreamed that his feet were stuck in the mud as he tried to scream a warning to the little girl in the red cotton dress.

No wonder Jesus said, *"...In this world you will have trouble. But take heart! I have overcome the world"* (John 16:33 NIV).

Your Reflections

_____

_____

_____

_____

_____

_____

_____

_____

_____

_____

_____

_____

_____

_____

_____

_____

_____

_____

_____

Reflections on *The Shack*

3

A CRISIS AVERTED

Shae

◇◇◇◇◇◇◇◇◇◇

A pull on a stuck pancake burns a hand. A simple wave hello tips a boat. A life-vest strap tangles in boat webbing and becomes a death trap. A last minute change of mind leads to a crisis. The crisis creates a diversion and a child disappears. Even the smallest seemingly insignificant details of our lives can influence outcomes; can lead to a chain of events that carry potential for calamity. More reason to be aware of God's presence in our lives. Sequences, however, can also lead to good outcomes.

Consider how quickly Mack, the children, and the campers gravitated toward one another. Those people would become a tremendous support when Missy disappears. And what of the circumstances of the calm night before, of his prayers of thanksgiving and then of Mack feeling what I deduce was a real sense of God's presence. "He was alone, yet not alone." For the most part, we have had a sense that he envied Nan's relationship with Papa, but here he is having his own experience with God and feeling "content."

We see its outcome the next morning as Mack senses that God and angels helped him succeed in rolling over the canoe and freeing his son, Josh. Did the Presence empower him for the first catastrophe? Mack not only released Emil from a "dam of pent up guilt and fear" about the canoe accident with a hug and kind words but also administered life-saving breath to Josh.

Donna
◇◇◇◇◇◇◇◇◇◇◇

"Before you cross the street, take my hand, life is just what happens to you, while you're busy making other plans." 1 John Lennon's striking words were written to his son Sean shortly before Lennon was gunned down.

Those many years ago, I saw John Lennon as a sort of rock 'n' roll sage. I no longer do. But he was an amazingly gifted artist. His song, "Beautiful Boy," was packed with poignancy and an eerie hint of prescience.

Like Lennon, Mack understands the fragility of life, even before he is tested by *The Great Sadness*. Mack's interaction with his children, his prayers of thanksgiving, even the fact that he bought Missy a "girlie" dress (how many dads would have opted for a more male-intuitive way to please their daughters?) seem to reveal his appreciation of life... and his determination to be fully present for every precious moment.

Poor Mack. He gave his kids a terrific weekend in the country, one they would always remember—campfires, sightseeing, you name it. Mack did more "dad-stuff" in one weekend than many kids experience in a lifetime. And in an act of fatherly love that should have capped off their perfect weekend, he saved his son's life! Yet, it was all about to go horribly wrong. The author telegraphs as much with his chilling chapter close: "A potential crisis had been averted. Or so Mack thought."

(Sigh) Prepare for *The Great Sadness*.

Endnote:

1. John-Lennon.com, "Beautiful Boy," http://www.johnlennon .com/songlyrics/songs/Beautiful_Boy_Darling_Boy.htm.

Tammy
◇◇◇◇◇◇◇◇◇◇◇

The beginning of this chapter may be the last time we have such a warm, fuzzy, innocent moment...and that foreboding feeling only enhances the peace around the campfire. The camaraderie of companionable strangers, the love of a family, and the hovering presence of God in nature all epitomize the proverbial "calm before the storm."

The next day introduces tragedy in a rapidly escalating pattern. Spilled pancakes and a burnt hand...it's OK, it's OK. Josh nearly drowns...but it's OK, it's OK. Then it hits—where is Missy? It's OK, it's OK...no. No it's not. We already know it won't be OK again for a very long time. Time to reach for the tissues and keep them close at hand, I fear.

Donna, I also like what you pointed out about how much wonderful "dad stuff" Mack is doing this weekend. I can feel the common question already rising: Why do bad things happen to good people? Especially a good guy like Mack and an innocent little girl like Missy. So many others have had similar experiences, and are still waiting for an answer.

Angela

Camping...not an activity I have ever wanted to explore. Not only are there sinister people lurking "out there" but also it's "nature where animals 'do things' on the ground" (as Monk would put it). I've heard from friends how much "fun" they have dragging food, tents, clothes, toiletries, and assorted stuff from their comfy cozy homes to a place in the mountains–but, ah, gee, that's just not my idea of fun.

Reading about Mack and his children hiking and enjoying the scenery is as close as I want to be to camping. And meeting up with other campers along the way reminds me of being trapped on a cruise ship with a zillion other people you don't know and have nothing in common with except you are all trapped on the same ship together...another activity I have never wanted to explore.

Hmmm...can you tell I'm getting a bit testy? I do not really want to relive or write about the part where Josh almost drowns. And Shae mentioned that Missy disappears? I'm wondering now why I started reading this book. As a mother I can't even allow my mind even one second to consider something tragic happening to one of my children or grandchildren. Blessed and/or cursed with being an overly empathetic person, I just don't even want to think about what may have happened to Missy. Maybe I'll skip over that part...

Your Reflections

_____

_____

_____

_____

_____

_____

_____

_____

_____

_____

_____

_____

_____

_____

_____

_____

_____

_____

A Crisis Averted

_____

_____

_____

_____

_____

_____

_____

_____

_____

_____

_____

_____

_____

_____

_____

_____

_____

_____

_____

_____

_____

_____

_____

_____

_____

_____

_____

_____

_____

4

THE LADYBUG

Donna

◇◇◇◇◇◇◇◇◇◇

Maybe—it's the word that staved off Mack's awful, looming reality for a few merciful moments before *The Great Sadness* was etched in stone.

As I read this chapter, I could feel the quaking of Mack's soul as multiple "maybes" poured out of the dialogue: "Maybe they're together....Maybe...[Missy] wandered away and got lost...maybe she...took a wrong turn...."

Mack's initial confrontation with terror is so extreme, I have nothing in my own life with which to compare it. There's the wintry night my doctor phoned with disappointing biopsy results. I'd had several weeks of "maybes" since the first tissue sample was tested: "Maybe it's nothing. Maybe there's an infection, or a cyst. Maybe the news is good and I will have dodged another bullet. Maybe—just maybe—my life won't be interrupted and irrevocably changed."

It's not the best memory on my highlight reel, but it's nothing like what Mack faced on that terrible day in the country. Mack had just one lifeline still tethered to Life As It Was Before Missy Vanished; it was the fraying thread of a "maybe": *Maybe Missy's alive and well playing hide and seek behind those trees, her red dress and sunny face smudged with child's play. Maybe I won't have to face the unbearable "what ifs" that will haunt me if she's been harmed.*

The ladybug pin snapped Mack's frayed thread of "maybes"—and, mercifully, his journey back to the real Lifeline was beginning.

Angela

As much as I didn't want to go...there I was right beside Mack as he, with hope, called Missy's name back at the campsite, as he ran to the rest area and searched frantically through the bathroom stalls and showers. I choked on the engorged lump in Mack's throat and felt his stomach churn with pain as he realized that she was gone. When he found the little red dress soaked in blood, I felt *The Great Sadness* descend on that loving father, and I cried for all the parents who have had to face this situation.

"If only" is an emotional (and sometimes spiritual) death sentence. Maybe Mack was so dead that the only way to get his attention was to send him a note. "Does God even write notes?" he wonders. I believe God will do whatever it takes to get our attention, to let us know He loves us more than we can ever imagine.

Mack's utter contempt for God is understandable, but so very sad. Although he was "sick of God and God's religion, sick of all the little religious social clubs...," surely he realized that "religion" and "religious social clubs" are humankind's inventions, not the intent of a loving and faithful heavenly Father.

Tragedy throws us into the arms of God whether we acknowledge His embrace or not.

Shae

The "what ifs" and "why" words always come later. Perhaps that's why after the tragedy, Mack ignored the growing sense of separation between he and God and tried instead to "embrace a stoic, unfeeling faith." However, that stone cold façade did not arrest the agony, stop the nightmares, or calm the screams of his heart to bring Missy back.

Why does God allow the gulfs that separate us from Him? What causes us to abandon God when we are deeply hurt? Why do we shut off our feelings in the midst of loss or pain? "I say to God my Rock, *'Why have you forgotten me?'* " (Psalm 42:9).

When my mother died in a fire, my heart cried— "Where were You God?" My sister in her battle with inoperable lung cancer— "God, YOU can do ALL things. You have the cure."

When my marriage broke apart— "God, You could have intervened..." His seeming lack of interest or involvement almost (forgive me Lord) made Him an indifferent perpetrator in my eyes and I created the gulf as a result. Slap me silly. Those tragedies should have reminded me of my utter need for God. Eventually, it was more painful and it took more strength to remain curled in a ball than the strength it took to reach out over the gulf, take God's outstretched hand, and strap myself to Him for the ride.

Mack will have to do just that. It's nearly four years later and he's about to meet God at the place of his deepest pain.

Tammy

After reading this chapter, I feel only one thing at the moment—I feel tired. It felt like days upon days of frantic, sleepless stress had piled up on me just as much as on Mack. I had to take breaks while I was reading, just to get a breather. Clearly, even the childless can identify on some level with a traumatic event like this.

Angela, I'm truly going to try to remember and take to heart what you said in your response to Mack's loathing for "all the little religious social clubs that didn't seem to make any real difference or effect any real changes"—you said this is a human creation, and not God's intention. My head knows that and agrees...maybe if I remind myself enough it'll sink into my heart eventually. Right now, my heart agrees with Mack.

I have seen *way* too much of "religious social clubs" in my short life so far, and I confess... (deep breath) I hate them. It seems like I can never truly fit in and be at home in them; all they ever do is shut me out.

Um, hehe, sorry. All that to just say I hear Mack loud and clear on that one, and I haven't even been through a tragedy like this.

Your Reflections

_____

_____

_____

_____

_____

_____

_____

_____

_____

_____

_____

_____

_____

_____

_____

_____

_____

_____

The Ladybug

_____

_____

_____

_____

_____

_____

_____

_____

_____

_____

_____

_____

_____

_____

_____

_____

_____

5

SURPRISE!

Angela

◇◇◇◇◇◇◇◇◇◇

OK...instead of talking about how Mack didn't tell his wife about the note in the mailbox and what he was going to do that weekend and how he contemplated suicide, I'm going straight for the obvious elephant in this chapter.

I was surprised to read that Mack was greeted inside the shack by God (Papa) who is a "large beaming African-American woman," and that the Holy Spirit was Sarayu, a "wiry-looking Asian woman." The "Middle Eastern man" dressed as a carpenter wasn't as much of a surprise.

I can only guess that because the author of *The Shack* was raised in New Guinea he may have encountered a large woman who was especially kind to him? Personally I've only ever thought of God as a larger-than-life being who is so loving that He meets each of His precious children no matter where, what, or who they are. His arms are always open to welcome all who believe.

I winced when Willie was sending off his friend Mack and said, "Well, if he does show, say hi for me." Why is it so hard for people to realize that God is only a whisper away, a thought away, a prayer away. Willie, like each person on this planet, has access to God every moment of every day through the saving grace of Jesus and our constant companion the Holy Spirit.

Tammy
◇◇◇◇◇◇◇◇◇◇

"Then again, why had he naturally assumed that God would be white?" Why indeed? After reading that line, whatever surprise I felt at the initial introduction of the Trinity sort of dissipated in what I can only call an "Oh" moment. I had forgotten that, globally speaking, I'm a serious ethnic minority.1 Given that realization, I have to smack my own forehead at how silly it was for me to ever restrict God in my imagination, making Him look more like me.

That, however, wasn't the most significant part of this chapter to me. The part I can't get over (because I love it) is when Mack first sees Papa...and she hugs the living daylights out of him and just keeps saying, "I love you!" Race and gender completely aside (as they should be), I couldn't stop grinning at that, thinking to myself, "That is so God." I also had to

smile at the three of them and their infectious laughter—
perfect.

What a blast, getting to meet these three (this One)! I can't
wait to spend the rest of the book in the company of a wonderful, relatable God like this!

Endnote:

http://anthro.palomar.edu/ethnicity/ethnic_5.htm.

Shae

Yes Tammy, we do tend to restrict God. Here the author
takes liberty through the genre of fiction to make the vital
point that God is not out there to take us down, that He is
approachable and loving. Young paints a portrait of an aspect
of God not unlike that of a mother hen brooding over her
chicks. Hey, who knew this was "chick" lit!

Mack needed spiritual refuge for his inner battle, a place where
he could rest, recover, and think clearly. The Bible says God
will shield us with His wings that God actually delights in
spreading them (see Ps. 91:4). We are encouraged to pour out
our hearts before Him, *"for God is our refuge"* (see Ps. 62:8).

Consider the wings of a doting mother hen, underneath is a
safe place its chicks can scurry to for protection and comfort.
The soft down sooths, her warmth envelops, and the steady
rhythm of her heart calms and reassures. We hear the sound
of God's own heart breaking with the tender fierce heart of a

mother, through Jesus' words, *"How often I would have gathered you, as a mother hen gathers her chicks...but you would not come"* (see Luke 13:34).

Mack has *finally* arrived at the gates of refuge, gates opened by his heart's inner desire to trust God enough to spill his heart. Somewhere in the midst of Mack taking that step of faith, God's wings extended—and Mack has found refuge. Eventually he'll reemerge to face the world again but for now, I think he's in a great place with Papa, as the doting and beaming mama hen. :^)

Donna
◇◇◇◇◇◇◇◇◇◇

Well! I certainly appreciate the author's ability to challenge paradigms with a compelling story. Imagining myself in Mack's shoes expands my horizons *and* forces me to search my own soul. In learning from and about others, I gain clarity about who I really am.

By positing a creative version of the Trinity, Wm. Paul Young challenges readers' notions of God. The construct served to uncover some ways in which I keep God in a box of my own making. I value that outcome. (I also applaud the outreach to people who have suffered great tragedies.)

With an unconventional presentation, Young made God's accessibility plain to the naked eye. Emotionally speaking, I found that touching; God *is* accessible and His accessibility is greatly underrated. On that count, kudos to Young! His point is well-crafted and well-taken.

But Young chose to present the Trinity. Therefore, his book implies Christianity and clearly places Mack in relationship, not with a generic god, but with the God of the Bible. So, while I agree that holding God in a Christian-ese box is to live in a stifling religious ditch, there's a ditch on the other side of the road, and that is to stretch what God has said about who He is.

I understand and appreciate artistic device, but I am uneasy with Young's artful presentation of the Godhead—and perhaps more concerned with its impact on impressionable readers. Biblically speaking, there is only one member incarnate of the Trinity.

So, turn the page, D.S., and let's try to keep the main thing the main thing.

Your Reflections

_____

_____

_____

_____

_____

_____

_____

_____

_____

_____

_____

_____

_____

_____

_____

_____

_____

Surprise!

_____

_____

_____

_____

_____

_____

_____

_____

_____

_____

_____

_____

_____

_____

_____

_____

REFLECTIONS ON *THE SHACK*

_____

_____

_____

_____

_____

_____

_____

_____

_____

_____

_____

_____

_____

_____

_____

_____

6

Pie, Anyone?

Angela

◇◇◇◇◇◇◇◇◇◇◇◇

Donna, I really appreciate your comments about God incarnate. I hope you will expand on that thought.

The Shack is an "unexpected" bestseller because an unknown author hits close to home for so many people. As he is talking to God, he blurts out, "If you couldn't take care of Missy, how can I trust you to take care of me?" I'm sure millions of people can relate to that statement in one context or another. It is natural to doubt; it is *supernatural* to rely on faith to make sense of the senseless. To make it in this world without crutches of alcohol, drugs, etc., we must have faith in the heavenly Father who loves us unconditionally.

Loved the scene in the kitchen. Many, many warm home-baked memories came rushing to my mind—my mother baking a pie for friends who were "just passing by," Daddy's coffee pot always full and ready to pour for a neighbor. Conversations light and serious took place around the kitchen table.

Mack was beginning to understand the love and nature of God in many different ways—far beyond what he learned in seminary. Like Tammy, many of us feel "shut out" of the religious boxes that are so tightly built these days. But there is no doubt that everyone is welcome and has a place at the table in the shack that God's builds!

Donna

Angela, for now I'm wading into *The Shack* carefully, appreciating the art, but being careful not to assimilate a concept of God that springs from man's creativity, be it the author's or my own.

I also enjoyed the kitchen scene. Like so many cultures, my Mediterranean heritage engenders kitchen appreciation. (lol!) Growing up, our kitchen was headquarters for everything from howling laughter to hurt feelings to homework. It was also where Mom produced the culinary and olfactory wonders that awakened us each Sunday morning. Ah, the mingled aromas of brewed coffee, sizzling bacon, fried meatballs, and simmering garlic-and-onion-tinged tomato sauce!

Somehow, kitchens help lower the walls of self-protection, even if only a little. I can imagine Papa, wooden spoon in hand, gazing out over her mixing bowl at a skeptical Mack;

it's the way my mother used to look at me when I sought a way around whatever well-seasoned wisdom she was dishing.

Papa knows Mack better than he knows himself. She (or is it "He"?) is whipping up the only sure-fire recipe for Mack's rescue—the healing of old wounds. Mack has been hanging precariously from the fraying thread of his own strength, but Papa knows what he really needs: to resolve the anger with his earthly father so he can learn to trust his heavenly Father.

Papa pinpoints the wound and sheds light on the cure saying: "If you let me, Mack, I'll be the Papa you never had." Wow— amazing love!

Shae

I am not a theologian but I sense a little loss in the area of reverence for God, and the glory of God. Is it just me?

My underlying concern as I delve deeper into the encounter with the Trinity is that those who do not know God's testimony of Himself in the Word and the awe one has as a result, will read some of Young's inaccurate concepts, as Donna alerted, as scriptural truth and accuracy.

Some people say *The Shack* has transformed them, that they read it over and over again. But what is so transforming, the author's own concepts? While I don't believe Mr. Young had a subversive theological agenda, I'm a tad concerned that some people will place the core message of Christianity into boxes constructed according to his ideals. Again it boils down to the confusion surrounding the work itself, is it fiction, or is it truth; what has biblical precedent and what doesn't?

We are most vulnerable when we are wounded. Cultists and New Agers know this—it is how they rope people into fabricated religions and beliefs. Not to say that this is a cult book, but it is vital that people read it through the lens of fiction, the author's intent, and with the Bible close by. It is a beautiful story and the upside is that it has become a vehicle for us to engage in conversations about the goodness and "love and nature of God," theology aside. And as far as I can see, the love of God *is* being shed abroad and promoted across many kitchen tables, and that message cannot be underrated, diluted, debated, or argued with in any way IMHO.

Tammy

Personally, I see nothing wrong with portraying the Three incarnate; to me, to say that it was only Jesus who was incarnate is to separate Him from the perfect unity He has with the other two. They are One; if one of them takes on a body, then all that God is has taken on a body.

On another note, I don't find this portrayal of God to lack reverence at all. I see how Papa, Jesus, and Sarayu relate to one another, and their expressions of love and enjoyment of each other *are* reverence...and it rubs off. I'm personally finding it easier to be awestruck by this beautiful, totally loving, and accessible view of God—it certainly beats some of the mental pictures I've had in the past.

Honestly, I think that for someone who doesn't know the Lord and is reading this book, this is not going to permanently convince them that God is just some friendly pal in the kitchen—that He isn't mighty and beyond us. The view of an inaccessibly holy, distant, omnipotent God is way more prevalent. The awesome and exciting thing is that, for the *many* people who have never thought of God as a Person with whom they can have an open, loving relationship, this book is ready to rock that notion and open their hearts to Him.

Your Reflections

_____

_____

_____

_____

_____

_____

_____

_____

_____

_____

_____

_____

_____

_____

_____

_____

_____

_____

Pie, Anyone?

7

So Simple, So Sincere

Angela
◇◇◇◇◇◇◇◇

Yes, Shae, I agree that's the rub—the thin line between fiction and God's living Word. While reading I keep waffling between being excited about such a "real" Trinity and the seeming lack of "reverence." Reading about Papa's bare feet took me immediately to the burning bush when God told Moses to remove his shoes because he was on holy ground (see Exod. 3:5). Yes, Tammy, reading *The Shack* as a non-believer would offer much comfort and is an excellent launching pad for jumping into a personal Christianity experience.

This chapter was filled with conflict within my spirit. I very much appreciated the three-in-one explanation regarding how they limit themselves out of respect for us—so beautiful. That concept was one I hadn't considered. Of course

God knows what we need before we need it, before we even ask for it, but He still wants us to ask Him, to talk with Him, to let Him love us.

Then when Mack was telling Jesus that he was not attractive, gee, how disrespectful is that?! Who would say that to another person, let alone your Savior?

Tammy
◇◇◇◇◇◇◇◇◇◇

I think artists throughout human history have already indirectly "told" Jesus the exact same thing, every time they paint Him. Personally, I don't see a lot of artists representing Him with all the odd facial quirks that usually accompany an "ordinary" look.

The time of devotion at the table was eye-opening for me. Something so simple, yet so sincere—it was nothing like what Mack had in mind when he heard the word "devotion." And, I must confess, I've been in on Mack-style devotions quite a few times.

This, however, truly made me consider the word itself: *devotion*. "Ardent, often selfless affection and dedication to a person; profound consecration"[1]—this doesn't describe some forced routine; this is a *way of life*. And, in the midst of such a life, a time of devotion doesn't need to be anything special— just a few minutes of pouring yourself out before the One you are devoted to.

Shae
◇◇◇◇◇◇◇◇◇◇◇

God "nose" all, lol Angela (groan)! Although elements of Chapter 7 are amazing, I am having trouble, even through my fiction lens, with the issue of God choosing to shrink to our level and limit Himself. Sarayu reminds Mack of an earlier conversation about choosing to limit oneself to honor a relationship and accomplish love. Sarayu explains that they (the Trinity) limit themselves in order to relate to Mack, out of respect for him. Recall the beginning quote of Chapter 6, by Jacques Ellul, author of *Anarchy and Christianity,* "...the first aspect of God is never that of the absolute Master, the Almighty. It is that of the God who puts himself on our human level and limits himself."

Hello. The first aspect of God is love, no? God *is* love. Love makes Him magnificent! If God was to limit Himself that would have to be limiting love, or am I missing something? Throughout the Bible, we see that He holds back nothing; that He doesn't *have* to lose anything or shrink any part of Himself to accomplish love. God Himself said that His thoughts are not ours, neither are our ways His. As the heavens are higher than the earth, so are His ways and thoughts higher than ours (see Isa. 55:8-9). I don't want God on my level—that would make Him very small indeed, and I don't want to serve a dwarfed or pint-sized god who submits to or is even likened one iota to wretched old corruptible me. I want/need Him cosmic big and uncompromising in my life! :^)

Donna
◇◇◇◇◇◇◇◇◇◇◇◇

Not wanting to beat this issue into fine dust, but isn't it terrific that a book can stir the waters and get the four of us (and countless other readers of *The Shack*) engaged in impassioned dialogue?

I hear you, Tammy and I don't want to throw out the baby with the bathwater. Still, I remain utterly conflicted about this book. My inner rocker relishes the thought of turning closed thinking inside out. The "me" who still has "the music" running through her veins can't help but shout, "Open the windows! Get yourself a front-row seat where you can see the realm of possibility without obstruction. Go ahead! Rock the boat. Jesus can handle it!"

And He can. It is refreshing to see Mack in open conversation with Father, Son, and Holy Spirit. Many people (a good percentage of whom have been beaten over the head with somebody's concept of "religion") would have a hard time believing such a relationship with God is possible. The construct of Young's Trinity can help them to *"taste and see that the Lord is good"* (Ps. 34:8 NLT).

Wonderful! But my concern involves the dark seed of relativism, the belief that "whatever works is OK." That creed has taken a toll on society. It does matter *how* you accomplish a worthy goal. Perhaps a preface from the author would have clarified the line between his marvelous allegory and straight-ahead biblical truth. Alas, advice that's a day late and a dollar short.^-^

Your Reflections

_____

_____

_____

_____

_____

_____

_____

_____

_____

_____

_____

_____

_____

_____

_____

_____

_____

_____

_____

_____

_____

_____

_____

_____

_____

_____

_____

_____

_____

_____

_____

_____

_____

REFLECTIONS ON *THE SHACK*

_____

_____

_____

_____

_____

_____

_____

_____

_____

_____

_____

_____

_____

_____

_____

_____

8

CIRCLE OF RELATIONSHIP

Shae
◇◇◇◇◇◇◇◇◇◇

Ka-ching! Kudos to Papa for explaining to Mack that while He doesn't like many of humanity's choices, His anger is an expression of love all the same. Anger is an expression of love—I tried to explain that to my then three-year-old son after he flushed my diamond watch down the toilet, when he scribbled his name all over my bathroom mirror with snot, and the day he hopped into the RV, shifted it out of park, and rolled it down the driveway almost into the neighbor's fence. Now that he just turned thirteen and is sowing rebellious oats, I remind him of my love at least twenty times a day!

Just as there can be righteous anger, I also believe that God is impatient in a good way—His impatience wrought by His genuine longing for relationship with us. His impatience for relationship with us is why Jesus gave His life at Calvary. I don't hear much Cross talk in this book; perplexing in a message meant to point people to the Love of God and to a place of forgiveness. The Atonement is the greatest act of love wrought on our behalf; where is the Wage and Gift message of Romans 6:23 and the Ultimate Love Message of John 3:16? I don't feel comfortable foraging it out of "God doesn't punish people for sin because sin is its own punishment." Chew on them greens!

Angela

Explaining away the lack of a "chain of command" and replacing it with a "circle of relationship" was hard for Mack to understand. Although hubby was 20 years in the U.S. Army where life and limb depended on authority and hierarchy, when it comes to spirituality, the circle of relationship defines it well.

As Christians we are called to be *in* the world but not *of* the world. Learning this as a child raised in the church by godly parents helped me keep major life things in perspective. Although I took prodigal detours (too many to mention in polite company) growing up, the solid-rock foundation kept me from blowing too far off course.

I wonder what seminary Mack attended that he didn't already realize this circle of relationship between the Trinity.

I don't understand why the concepts in the conversation in this chapter seems so foreign to Mack. Maybe an explanation to a non-believer who stumbled into the shack would be necessary, but to a man who had attended seminary and church? Hmmm... (angela)

Tammy
◇◇◇◇◇◇◇◇◇◇◇

"We're not justifying it. We are redeeming it." Far as I see, that's exactly what God is in the business of doing here in human history. Certainly, the Bible talks about a Day of Judgment coming—I think Mack's picture of a punishing God comes partly from this—but you know, from Jesus onward, all I see in the Bible is redemption...until the very end.

In the meantime, sin really is its own punishment. I have no problem with Papa saying that at all—that truth is painfully obvious to me. I guess you could say that, for a non-believer to really get a full picture (and be warned), the author should have made it clear that God would be the Judge someday... but once again, this is fiction, not a theological treatise. As such, that kind of side note ("Oh, I love you, and by the way, I'm gonna burn you all with My wrath someday, honey") doesn't fit in this story.

Some may not think that's enough to make the seriousness of sin clear to non-believers, but I disagree. Talk of wrath and punishment, to me, isn't the way to explain that to people anyway—it's just a scare tactic. Showing them the havoc sin wreaks in their own lives is a good start. Best of all, though, is showing them the price Jesus was willing to pay to cleanse us of it...and Papa already showed Mack some of that, in the terrible scars She and Jesus share.

Donna
◇◇◇◇◇◇◇◇◇◇

You gals make such intriguing observations! My mind is bouncing from one to the other like the silver sphere in a pinball machine. Then *tilt!* There it is! A political junkie's quip du jour: the passage Shae already mentioned. After Mack spills his guts about Papa's supposed "great bowls of wrath," Papa replies in part: "I don't need to punish people for sin. Sin is its own punishment, devouring you from the inside."

That's an artful, Beltway-type answer. But, two points stick out like Alfalfa's cowlick. *Of course* sin devours from within. An atheist or two might agree with Papa on that one! But it's a red herring which distracts from the issue of whether, from God's perspective, sin has a price. And Papa's careful wording "I don't *need* to punish people..." (emphasis added) continues the deflection. Outwardly, Young portrays a kinder, gentler Papa than Mack had in mind. But if you follow Papa's statement to its logical conclusion, she could be passive-aggressive. Instead of confronting the sin issue, Young's Papa seems content to kick the can down the road and let those doggone sinners self-destruct...without so much as Papa's fingerprint on the body.

Were it true, Mack would be right—God is downright mean. Instead the Father says, "Hey, I love you too much not to tell you the truth. The price of sin is death, but I have a solution: it's called the Cross. My Son did it just for you" (see Rom. 6:23).

That's my Daddy—hands-on and heart full of love!

Your Reflections

_____

_____

_____

_____

_____

_____

_____

_____

_____

_____

_____

_____

_____

_____

_____

_____

_____

Circle of Relationship

9

WHAT A GARDEN!

Shae
◇◇◇◇◇◇◇◇◇◇

Whoa, brilliant moments! Imagine how Mack felt when he discovered that the haphazard but exquisite garden of colorful flowers and poisonous plants Sarayu took him through was *his soul*. Sarayu also shares the account of The Great Sorrow Day in the garden of long ago that "tore the universe apart, divorcing the spiritual from the physical." Adam and Eve thought they had a right to the Tree, but they thought wrong, and in their choice to sample its fruit, lost supernatural sight and closeness with the Creator of the Universe. Mack's Great Sadness, their Great Sorrow, it all ties together in a beautiful way with an incredible outcome. The Atonement and the following precious gift of the Presence of the Holy Spirit help us once again "see" from God's perspective what we don't see in the natural realm. Peering through heavenly lenses is sort of like tracking a storm by satellite picture, whereby we can see and know its direction, its strength, its anticipated impact, where the eye is, and what we can do to either ride through it or circumnavigate it.

The Holy Spirit walks me through that garden of chaos, too. Many hurts hide deep beneath its earthen floor. But God has exhumed fragrant hope for me there; unearthing purpose, healing, and beauty in the pain, suffering, and ugly. Here, we also inter things that hinder our walking on water together. I wonder if Mack is yet aware that the spot they are clearing in the garden resembles a burial plot.

Angela

Oh how I loved walking through the Monet-Giverny-type flower garden with Mack and Sarayu. My flower beds bring me much peace and joy—there is nothing more fun than playing in the dirt. (Well, playing in the sand at the ocean ranks a close second.)

Realizing that the messy garden was actually Mack's soul was beautiful. And realizing that my messy soul is actually being groomed and pruned by my heavenly Father brings an even more restfulness to my spirit. Isn't that just like God? Whenever you think you know Him, He does something or causes you to realize something that brings you even closer to Him. I just love that!

What I don't always love, though, is the "clearing away" and the "uprooting" that must take place from time to time. Many of the flowering shrubs and trees that we planted 20 years ago when we had our home built are now looking straggly and old. When we dug some out and replaced them, I felt sad...still do. I miss the familiar landscape, but I eventually learned to appreciate the freshness and vibrancy of the new plantings. I pray that I will learn to appreciate the new plantings God is blessing me with daily.

P.S. Shae, I'm surprised that you didn't comment about your likeness to Mack's wife in his comment about how it was hard to keep up with Sarayu—like "trying to follow Nan in a mall." (ha!)

Donna
◇◇◇◇◇◇◇◇◇◇◇

"Your question presumes that poison is bad; that such creations serve no purpose." Sarayu set a few paradigms on edge with that stunner. I say "stunner" not because the statement is in any way a stretch. Everyone's got a bottle of bleach under the cabinet. It's a poison with a purpose and we use it to our advantage.

Sarayu's statement is arresting because, for the world to make sense to us, the words *poison* and *bad* must remain linked. If the link is broken at the wrong time (during childhood, for example) you could become a very young, but very dead duck. *Poison. Bad.*

Even now, if you want me to believe poison is good for me, you're going to have to give me an iron-clad argument. Still, the argument will apply only in the rarest of circumstances. Case in point: "Donna, this chemo cocktail will knock you for a loop, but it does a great job of incinerating bad cells."

OK. I get that. Another layer of God's goodness is revealed through something completely counter-intuitive. The poison wasn't an accident—He created it with a purpose in mind! And the relational weirdness that happened after my recovery? It felt an awful lot like a knife in my heart, but it helped me to take a great leap forward in my destiny journey. God knew that!

Missy's death. The Great Sadness. For Mack, the terms had become inseparable. But the link is coming undone.

Tammy
◇◇◇◇◇◇◇◇◇◇

To tell the truth, I strongly dislike gardening. I find it to be unpleasantly dirty, hard work. I guess that makes the analogy all the more spot-on for me, as Mack and Sarayu work in the garden of his soul. Dealing with my own internal issues can be as daunting a task as gardening to me.

That's why I found it particularly comforting to realize, at the end of the chapter, just how beautiful the interaction was throughout. Sarayu and Mack worked *together,* side-by-side, on clearing the ground in his soul. She didn't sit back and make him do all the work, but neither did she take care of everything for him. She worked and he worked, they helped each other, and in the meantime they shared conversation and fellowship.

It makes the prospect of facing my own inner garden a little less frightening to realize that the Holy Spirit is right there with me, sharing the work and sharing the time together, and that He has a design in mind for me that is a colorful, intricate mess. I think I can get my hands dirty for a project like that. ^_^

Your Reflections

_____

_____

_____

_____

_____

_____

_____

_____

_____

_____

_____

_____

_____

_____

_____

_____

_____

_____

What a Garden!

_____

_____

_____

_____

_____

_____

_____

_____

_____

_____

_____

_____

_____

_____

_____

10

A Visual Symphony

Shae

◇◇◇◇◇◇◇◇◇◇

Nan, Sarayu, and I will get along just fine. :^) BTW. Wouldn't it be interesting to hear the story from Nan's POV?

Way cool time here with Jesus. Just when we are sinking in quicksand (and up to our ears in credit card debt!), He comes along and offers us a walk on the wild side of faith. Our mission, if we accept, is to place our feet atop the cold water and trust that He won't desert us in the middle of the lake *vis* our future, which looks rather dismal today to many people experiencing tough economic times.

Did fear fuel the outcome of the U.S. election? Smack in the middle of the campaign for presidential office, the stock market plummeted, life savings went "poof!" and hundreds of thousands of people lost their homes, their jobs. Millions grieved over the death of more brave soldiers and the discovery of toddler Caylee Anthony's remains in Florida.

People placed their hope in Barack Obama to save the nation and turn things around. Consider this. A recent interactive Harris poll asked 2,634 Americans who they admire enough to call a hero. President Obama, who hasn't done much yet, topped the poll. Jesus came in second, and God ranked 11th *ouch* between Mother Teresa and Hillary Clinton. Interestingly, a similar poll in 2001 placed Jesus at the top.[1]

Can one man save a nation? Not unless His name is Jesus, and millions of people are getting their feet wet with Him.

Endnote:

Fox News, February 21, 2009: Report accessed February 25, 2009; http://www.foxnews.com/politics/first100days/2009/02/21/poll-obama-popular-jesus-gandhi-king/

Angela
◇◇◇◇◇◇◇◇◇◇◇

I was so glad that Mack didn't sink beneath the waters (like Peter did) as he was walking on the lake with Jesus. Obviously his faith is getting stronger and deeper as he spends more time with the Trinity.

I was intrigued with the statement that "without wisdom, imagination is a cruel taskmaster." I'd add "without *God's revelatory* wisdom...." Our imaginations can provide the most beautiful scenes or the most horrible schemes. Surrendering our existence to Him allows His will to be accomplished.

As Mack was "grinning ear to ear just thinking about what he was doing" as he walked across the lake, I too experienced a similar giddiness when my husband and I took a helicopter ride over the active volcano on Hawaii's Big Island recently. Like Mack we too saw a beautiful waterfall spilling over a cliff's edge on the way toward the lava-spewing crater. I may not have been walking on water with Jesus, but I know He was with me as I mustered courage to stepped into that small aircraft and sat cheek-to-cheek with the pilot.

As Mack talked with Jesus about relationships, power, and the roles males and females have, I remembered the day—the moment—I gave God complete power over my life. Being a relatively conservative (well, *mostly* conservative) person, I was scared that He might want me to do something outrageous. He never has. But as I grow deeper in His love for me—I'd gladly do something completely shocking for Him.

Tammy
◇◇◇◇◇◇◇◇◇◇◇

I find that funny, Angela, considering *my* fear was actually that His plan for me would be something completely *normal.* ^_^

This chapter was simply packed with stuff I thought was great. I found the talk about submission simply revelatory, not to mention marvelously comforting. I have to say, I grew up being taught that "Wives, submit to your husbands," and "Husbands, love your wives" means the man is in charge and the woman must submit...and I have *never* liked that one bit (see Eph. 5:22-25). (It might be another reason I've stayed single!) But this idea of relationship makes so much more sense to me, and it is truly beautiful—two people, both living submitted to each other and to God in love. It's a breath of fresh air to me to hear submission explained this way.

Right before the end, there's another gem too—the idea that Jesus didn't live His life as a model for us to copy...because, through our efforts, we never *could*. Instead, He just wants to live inside of us, and by having Him living freely within us, His life becomes ours and our lives are lived to please Him. And again, I smack my forehead and think, "Duh! That sounds so much simpler than what I was thinking!" ^_^

Donna
◇◇◇◇◇◇◇◇◇◇

How I wish I could say there was a specific day when I gave God complete power over my life. For me, it's a painstaking—and yes!—joy-producing process. My journey is highlighted by major control-releasing milestones; but it's more often marked by incremental shifts in my woefully flawed thinking.

I am thankful for those paradigm-busting days when I leap at Jesus' invitation to walk on the water with Him—days when I run full-throttle to the lake's edge and glide confidently across waves of adversity...doubt...resistance. But those breakthroughs always prove to be a letting go of a *certain amount* of control; it's the amount I'm aware I'm hoarding.

No sooner do my clothes drip dry on the opposite shore that I discover another layer of control waiting to be released. That's when the waters in my rear-view mirror begin to look choppier, more threatening, harder to cross. Like Mack, I mumble to Jesus, "I have so far to go." Then I look into His knowing eyes and ask, "Will You walk me across yet another gulf?"

Today is one of those days. The wind is blowing across the lake with unnerving intensity. The scene, usually lush and inviting, seems more grey, more forbidding. I'd rather queue up a Cary Grant movie and a bucket of popcorn than don my timeworn rubberized shoes and commit to another bad hair day on the high seas of heart transformation. But Jesus beckons...and His love is calling me forward.

Please send hairspray. :-)

Your Reflections

_____

_____

_____

_____

_____

_____

_____

_____

_____

_____

_____

_____

_____

_____

_____

_____

_____

_____

_____

_____

_____

_____

_____

_____

_____

_____

_____

_____

_____

_____

_____

_____

_____

11

JUDGMENT IN DISGUISE

Shae

◇◇◇◇◇◇◇◇◇◇◇

Trauma exists regardless of "why" or "how." What a relief to know "God turns things to good," rather than, "God will make bad things happen to bring about good." While at first it was hard to see how God could possibly turn Missy's brutal death to any benefit, here we see how He has through the softening of Mack's heart. It all resonates with the gist of Job's plight. As Mack has, Job's first reaction was to doubt and question God's nature through blame; judgment in disguise. In essence, *why are You doing this to me...it is not fair!* Assigning blame temporarily satisfies until God asks, "Who are you to judge or blame anyone, at fault or not?" God's purpose in the Book of Job, and what I believe the whole point of *The Shack* to be, is not the *promise* of a pot of gold—of reward or benefit at the end of our suffering but *in the* reward of comprehending the Father love of God and the fullness of His true nature. Consequently, we discover who we are in Him as His beloved and precious children. This, in turn, transforms our beliefs about suffering, the cure for Plank-in-Eye Disease perhaps!

Interestingly, in both cases the intensity of the awfulness of their suffering resulted in a supernatural revelation of intense goodness. IMHO, Mack could not have endured seeing Missy through the waterfall—not being able to hold her, without at least a smidgen of this truth cradled in his heart.

Angela

◇◇◇◇◇◇◇◇◇◇◇◇

I think Chapter 11 is the most profound chapter so far. Realizing that when we judge others (no matter how heinous the offense) we are ultimately judging God, our True Love and Provider, was a gut-grabbing revelation.

"How far do we go back, Mackenzie? This legacy of brokenness goes all the way back to Adam, what about him? ...God started this whole thing. Is God to blame?"

God's original intention was to create beings with whom He could share His world, beings to commune with—to bless and enjoy and love. God's only intention was to set us (Adams and Eves) up in a perfect Garden with all the beauty, food, warmth, shelter, and an eternity of love to fill every morsel of every day.

Instead we allowed evil to tempt and corrupt us. For this, punishment is required. Thank you, Jesus, for serving our life sentence, for redeeming us. For the crimes we commit to others, punishment is required. I must have faith that child molesters and killers of the innocent will be punished. God is the ultimate judge—not me, not Nancy Grace, not some slick lawyer who finds a loophole—only God.

Only God can mete out the kind of justice we all deserve. I don't think justice based on love is within our power. Our "good intentions" are so tainted through corrupt perceptions that we can't always trust how to "set things right." But there is One who can always be counted on to judge with love.

Tammy
◇◇◇◇◇◇◇◇◇◇◇

I still don't see the absence of God's role as Judge to be suggesting that He isn't one, or will never judge sin. I think it comes down to how we read into a story about our God. We know God, we know the many ways He works and roles He has, and we expect to see *all* of that fairly represented. If we don't, we begin to suspect that the author is saying something false about God.

However, I don't think this is the case. I think this chapter on judgment is about Mack, and his human nature to place himself above others. It's an entirely different thing from divine judgment, and we're not looking at that aspect of God here. What we do learn about Papa is the depth of Her love, and we get an analogy to help us understand why She and Jesus chose to extend grace to humanity.

Does this mean there will never be judgment? No. I don't see the author saying that at all. Once again, this is a novel, and judgment is still to come. In the meantime, God is working His grace and love into human history, seeking to share relationship with every individual. *This* is the God Mack needs to know fully, and *this* is the God so many in our world today have never heard of. It's the message of the whole book—I hope everyone will hear it.

Donna

◇◇◇◇◇◇◇◇◇◇

Mack's trip to the cave was an emotional roller-coaster. The highs and lows were intense. Mack's incendiary anger flared and then dissolved into a cool puddle at the base of the waterfall.

Mack is not a quitter. He took on this wild cave ride like a cowboy takes on a bucking bronco. He'd come too far to quit the rodeo; so he just let the bronc rip. By the time his ride was over, I clutched *my* neck to make sure it was still in one piece.

Surely God's grace carried Mack through the cave experience. What else could? (Reading about the moment he traced his rage back to God rocked me and shook free some of my own memories.) And how freely he rejoiced when Missy hugged him from across the divide; it was a powerfully poignant moment!

Still, this chapter raised more questions for me, like *Who was that mystery woman?* (She may have given a hint as to her identity when she said she was "especially fond" of Misty, but that just creates more questions.) And was she suggesting that there is no judgment with God?

Like Mack in the cave; confronting *The Shack* (the book, that is) lights up both ends of my emotional and cognitive spectrum. I love good storytelling and some of the message points are well taken. But there's a fluid subtext that I'm not so sure about. I'm just eating the meat and spitting out the bones.

Your Reflections

_____

_____

_____

_____

_____

_____

_____

_____

_____

_____

_____

_____

_____

_____

_____

_____

_____

_____

Judgment in Disguise

_____

_____

_____

_____

_____

_____

_____

_____

_____

_____

_____

_____

_____

_____

_____

_____

_____

_____

12

LOST AND FOUND

Shae

Not that I'm fixated on bones...lol. Ouch! I expected greater things of this chapter following the lifting of Mack's Great Sadness and his reconciliation with the Lord. The author could have nailed the One Way message here IMHO but instead used valuable space to soapbox the institutional evils of religion, politics, and economics. While Mack seems to have let go of his Great Sadness, there seems an underlay of hurt and things the author himself still cannot let go of or still casts blame to that perhaps has hardened his heart to the point of being anti, anti, anti what he perceives has dealt him wrong cards.

I was taken aback by Jesus' explanation to Mack that Missy was never alone, that they were there through the brutality. Of course

Mack had trouble taking it all in—what parent wouldn't? If it were my child, even in light of all of the explanations thus far from God, it would raise the question afresh in my mind, "You are so loving and kind, how could you sit back and watch?" As a parent, I'd be tearing her away from that madman's clutch... Oh my—I'm still a piece of work...do I really believe Jesus' presence is enough?

Burrs and blurs aside, I was deeply moved by the picture of Mack weeping in Jesus' arms. It resonates, "There was reclining on Jesus' breast one of His disciples, whom Jesus loved." What a leap for Mack and what a coup for Jesus. I am sure Sarayu was close by with her tear bottle.

Tammy
◇◇◇◇◇◇◇◇◇◇◇

I must say, I don't see a soapbox here—I see a consistent message that emphasizes a love relationship with God above everything else. Papa, Jesus, and Sarayu have been showing Mack this from the beginning, but why stop now? Now that *The Great Sadness* has lifted, Mack can begin to hear with new clarity. In addition, I am very glad that the author makes this specific point—a relationship with God does not mean you then have to get deeply involved in religion, do the "church thing" for the rest of your life, or conform to any human standard. Church, while not all bad by any means, is a major sticking-point for many unbelievers...believers too. They need to hear the message that it's OK—they aren't left out in the cold or denied God's acceptance just because they don't fit the Christian bill.

I'm thrilled to see the author making this point, and I feel it fits wonderfully in the flow of the story right now. It's exactly what misfitted, church-wary believers and unbelievers alike need to hear—I should know, I'm one myself, and the reminder was like a breath of fresh air to me.

Heaven forbid anyone hear a message like, "Once you're a Christian, you'll fit right in." For different reasons, I think that's almost as bad a lie as "All roads lead to Heaven." Instead, we hear Jesus saying, "I will travel any road to find you." Perfect, and perfectly true.

Donna

◇◇◇◇◇◇◇◇◇◇◇

Oh, Tammy, that line is such a heart-opener! And it *is* perfectly true. I often think about where Jesus "found" me; it encourages my faith about where He's willing to go for others. I also find myself agreeing with both you and Shae about Mack's views of the Church and religion.

As a teen, I found myself standing on the wrong end of "religion." I remember thinking, *That's it! I will never set foot in a church again...*and I didn't, at least not for a couple of decades. The experience that triggered my vow was humiliating and infuriating.

So I "get" Mack's skepticism. But I also know how easy it is to broad-brush the deal. In the days since I broke my youthful vow, I've waded back into spiritual community. Yes, I have experienced ups *and* downs. Being a "continuing single" in the Church has been a challenge for me. But my union with the (imperfect) Church has yielded countless God-inspired outcomes in my heart and life—whether through the pulpit, a mentoring moment, a casual conversation, or those moments of revelation in the Spirit-soaked atmosphere of corporate worship.

When I went through a catastrophic illness, the Church rallied to my side. Errands were run, rides were provided, meals were prepared. People who didn't even know me saved my bacon...when I couldn't save my own.

Through the Church I also get to love others—both inside and outside its walls. I've come to appreciate that...big time.

Angela

To some degree it sounds like we are all singing the same off-key tune about our past "religious and church" experiences. But don't you think we are hiding our real feelings behind saying "religion" left us high and dry or "the church" left us bewildered? Let's shoot from the hip. Church people don't treat us as expected. We think that walking into a church miraculously changes people into saints. Not so.

What we encounter (sometimes if not most times) are cliques that won't let you in because you don't pray aloud the way they do, or you want to raise your hands in praise, or you don't bring the right dish to the potluck dinners. (OK, I'm exaggerating about the right dish.) But really, don't we have a sour taste because some of the people who attend church are judgmental, hypocritical, harsh, and down-right mean? Yes, I'm speaking from experience.

That's why when you actually come to know Jesus as your very own personal Savior, it is a feeling and knowledge so deep and so comforting that you know that you know He is the only person who can ever bring you total peace and love.

We are all works in progress—souls full of messy gardens. Treating others as He would have us treat them is a great start to providing God the good PR He deserves.

Yea for Donna's church family who "gets it!" With the grace of God, may others get it too.

Your Reflections

_____

_____

_____

_____

_____

_____

_____

_____

_____

_____

_____

_____

_____

_____

_____

_____

_____

_____

Lost and Found

_____

_____

_____

_____

_____

_____

_____

_____

_____

_____

_____

_____

_____

_____

_____

13

IF THE SHOE FITS

Shae

◇◇◇◇◇◇◇◇◇

Ah, now we get into the subject of grace and of how it does not depend on suffering to exist but that it is there in our suffering. Papa describes it as not always appearing as we expect it to, that we will find it "in many facets and colors." The most obvious place to find it is at the Cross; in Christ's suffering, the message of grace is clearly written in scarlet.

In this meeting of hearts, Mack could have taken offense to Papa who essentially labeled him as stupid and an idiot but instead shrugged it off and planted a kiss on Papa's cheek. Mack loves God, no doubt! I could shrug it off too as "Man, open your eyes to the work of Calvary—the ultimate act of sacrificial love." More marred was Jesus than any man. Nails punctured, thorns pierced, whips ripped, blood gushed, and still He could say, "Forgive them Father." Indeed, what further proof do *I* need of His love? Yet at times, I *still* create great gulfs between us. Slap me silly Father for I have sinned. Call *me* blonde, I deserve it. (SHAE)

Donna

◇◇◇◇◇◇◇◇◇◇◇

If the shoe fits? This shoe is one-size-fits-all!

Papa provides so much insight into our humanity that I have to keep re-reading passages. The one I'm parked on right now has to do with God's omniscience, the idea that He knows how many times I'm going to walk around the same old mountain in my one-size-fits-all blister-bakers. So while I chase my tail in exhausting circles and kick myself for being an idiot *again,* He sees my convoluted path as being strangely on course—as though it were stretched out as the crow flies.

Imagine seeing the end from the beginning and being free to happily count off the circular journeys without frustration! *That* is freedom. The contrast between God's point of view and my own is equivalent to the difference between night and day. For some reason, Papa's conversation with Mack cements that for me and highlights the Father's complete clarity in the midst of craziness.

Instead of shaking His head in disbelief at my idiotic choices, He cheers me on. Such love! As I ponder it, a melody rises from within me...it's from the song "Amazed" by Jared Anderson. The lyrics that come to mind speak to this idea of the Father rooting for us: "You dance over me while I am unaware...You sing all around but I never near the sound."1

Our coveted independence is worth nothing compared to His love—and I want to *always* hear His singing.

Endnote:

1. Jared Anderson, "Amazed," © 2004 Vertical Worship Songs.

Shae

Boy, I gotta tell you, I found this chapter so liberating. The way Papa explained Her point of view on human failings was such a relief. I grew up hearing a lot of Ephesians 4:30, *"Do not grieve the Holy Spirit of God."* I came to look at all my repeated failures as me disappointing a perfect God of love, again and again and again. I guess I didn't so much see Him as angry with me...more like just brokenhearted all the time.

What a freeing thought then, to realize that maybe God *isn't* sitting up there, watching me mess up with an eternal frown of sorrow on His face. I'm beginning to realize just how much that false idea of God held me up—fear that He's disappointed in me certainly puts a barrier on unrestrained love. And what a time-waster guilt is! When I could be picking myself up and moving on to the next lesson, I've such a tendency to sit there kicking myself over my mistakes.

Realizing that God isn't held up by my failings is such a wonderful feeling, like a lovely spring breeze. And just like Mack,

I don't mind being called an idiot in the least...it's true, and He loves me anyway, so why not? I can just see Papa shaking Her head and calling me blonde. How wonderful! ^_^

Angela
◇◇◇◇◇◇◇◇◇◇

Knowing that God's love is greater than our stupidity is so very comforting. It sums up God's faithfulness throughout the ages. When the first two just had to eat from that tree, when people kept whining for a king, when people were shouting to let Barabbas go, when crusaders killed other believers, when a dictator's army slaughtered millions of God's chosen people, when doctors murder the unborn...God's love is greater.

And for me—there are not enough pages in a book to list all of the stupid, idiotic things I've done, said, thought, or imagined. Yet Jesus never forsakes me. His redeeming grace brings me back to a place of loving reproof and gentle conviction. I fall at His feet not because I feel condemned but because I want to make it right with Him.

Reading what you wrote, Tammy, reminded me of people I know who have a constant underlying feeling of guilt that was planted there when they were youths being raised in a strict religious environment. There is a fine line between guilt and grace-full conviction. I wonder if *The Shack* has been so successful because it is so liberating and reconciling for people suffering from this heavy burden.

Your Reflections

_____

_____

_____

_____

_____

_____

_____

_____

_____

_____

_____

_____

_____

_____

_____

_____

_____

_____

14

LIVING TRUTH

Angela

◇◇◇◇◇◇◇◇◇◇

Knowing that the Trinity is always with me can be problematic. When I'm happy and content and things are going my way—yippee—Jesus and I skip to my Lou my darling. But when I want to respond "unpleasantly" to an irritating colleague or stubborn family member, I tend to push Him into a closet until I'm over my little temper tantrum.

I know God isn't just Someone who appears on Sunday mornings; I know that He is constantly with me. I know He is speaking to me about how I should react to situations, how He is continuing to shape my messy flower garden, how He wants me to praise and worship Him for His goodness, truth, and mercy. In my home sweet home comfort zone, I'm so OK with that. But it is another story when I'm out in the world with others.

As peaceful as Mack was paddling out on the lake, he realized that he would have to return to his life away from the shack. Leaving the shack doesn't mean leaving God, it means moving forward toward the Truth of life. We all struggle at times with our emotions. I'd venture to say that there are more people on medication for depression now than ever before. The evil one uses people's emotions to trick them into focusing on things other than the One who can bring them ultimate peace.

Donna
◇◇◇◇◇◇◇◇◇◇◇

Mack is in information overload! Of course, he has the likes of the Trinity to help him sort it out. Still, having a lifelong belief system overwritten in a day would have to leave a guy like Mack (or a gal like me) wondering which way is up.

Digesting this "session over dinner" is proving to be an incremental process. It's the gastric equivalent of serving a 12-course feast to someone who just had lap-band surgery. Sarayu's discourse regarding responsibility (as opposed to response) and expectation (as opposed to expectancy) is enough to bust a lap-band-less gut over.

As Mack's head began to spin, cracks began appearing in the walls of my own fortresses of mis-belief. A video began running in my head and it wasn't particularly pretty. The images didn't rise to the level of horror or horribleness (my word, thank you :-)), but the footage did reveal instances in which my own lust for certainty (hidden in my blind spot though it was) played out in petty ways, sometimes at the expense of others.

It takes the form of expectation that people (myself included) will do the "right" thing. Duh...isn't that the way it's supposed to be? Yet I realize that my concept of the right thing is at least partly subjective—and even the parts that are based in sound absolutes can impose a stuffy deadness on living relationships.

Time to re-think some things. Maybe even my theological concerns about this book?

Maybe...maybe not.

Shae

Overload is right Donna! Questions, questions! Mack asks so many questions of God.

For the longest time I did not *dare* question my gavel-toting Father for fear of a lightning strike. Who was I, a Blonde Skinny Speck, to question the Vast Creator of Color; the very Author of The Universe on any matter pertaining to "why" or "how come?" I had questions—truck loads of 'em about life and even about what I read in the Bible but no place to dump for fear of wrath or repercussion.

Enter the Holy Spirit Who beamed the awe and wonder, approachability and love of the Living God into my life—and welcomed questions—no matter the wounding, bitterness, or outright naïveté provoking them. Voicing what was deepest in my heart: questions, struggles, even doubts; grew my faith, my humility, and my spiritual life. I no longer searched inside myself but to the Precious One who lives inside of me to bring about answers not of man-made syllables, dots, or tittles; but of heart words—an inner language of kaleidoscopic revelation that even brought life to the Bible's "begats" and "begottens." No longer did I have to figure things out for myself—what freedom that is for a blonde!

His very nature is that my asking one question begs for another, and then truths build upon truths, precepts upon precepts in my heart, every answer leading to deeper questions, leading to greater revelation of His Person and deepening relationship with the Living Answer—which brings true Living Color into my life minus the burden of overload, which of course causes grey!

Tammy
◇◇◇◇◇◇◇◇◇◇◇

I have to admit, I had way too much fun with this chapter. God is a verb, and I'm a word nerd who gets a major kick out of that. ^_^

I also had my curiosity piqued when Sarayu said that the word "responsibility" wasn't in the Scriptures. I had to see that for myself. I found that it's not *quite* true—some versions use it more frequently, but most versions have at least a few places where the word crops up. However, the only verses that use the word consistently are in the Old Testament, in the Law. I found very little in the Bible to hint at God placing a responsibility on people, which was Sarayu's point.

Instead, there's just so much to respond to! More than you could live out in a lifetime, in fact. And that's another cool thing about this—a responsibility doesn't take that long. You do it, perform your duty or keep the rule, and you're done. A *response,* however, might end up carrying on forever, like a conversation between two close friends. My response to some aspect of God can lead Him to respond right back with some new side of Himself, pulling a new answer from me...and on and on we can go, for as long as I live and beyond.

Responsibility is dry, one-way, and soon ended. But responding to God will never die out too soon or leave awkward pauses in the conversation. It's an eternal way of living.

Your Reflections

_____

_____

_____

_____

_____

_____

_____

_____

_____

_____

_____

_____

_____

_____

_____

_____

_____

_____

_____

_____

_____

_____

_____

_____

_____

_____

_____

_____

_____

_____

_____

_____

15

Colorful Imagining

Donna

◇◇◇◇◇◇◇◇◇◇

Imagine seeing what Mack saw and then reverting to natural vision. As I search my memory bank for something to which I can compare Mack's experience (somewhat), I begin to recall stories of people who've had so-called "near-death experiences." (I say *so-called* because, according to their doctors or attending paramedics, some of these people had literally died.)

Over the years, I've come across many such stories. (Haven't we all?) Some of those who were "brought back" describe leaving their bodies, hovering over their deathbeds or the scene of the accident in which they perished, and going to Heaven. Several have talked about how amazing Heaven is and how great they felt being there. One or two spoke soberly about God sending them back into their bodies to accomplish a certain ministry work or other assignment on the earth.

All of these people describe the bittersweet prospect of having to leave Heaven—including those who had beloved spouses and even children praying for them to be revived! Being in Heaven was so perfect that the thought of going back to life on earth seemed entirely unattractive and seriously anticlimactic.

I guess Mack, who got a sneak peak at the natural world through a supernatural peephole, felt much the same way. Yet, I'm sure he wouldn't have traded the experience for anything. And I can only imagine the restorative value of his brief, yet powerful reconnection with his dad—like a long, cool drink to a parched section of his soul, no doubt.

Shae

Juxtapose the "hell" Mack went through with that of his heaven-meeting-earth-to-touch-his-pain experience—and yes—having once again to "see" by faith would be a difficult adjustment. However, through relationship with the fullness of God, Mack doesn't peer through the glass darkly anymore— the chronic spiritual monochromatic myopia is gone—he can see through rainbow-hued glasses what he couldn't before—hope in hopelessness, sense in senselessness, and life in death.

Sure, sure, he'll beg for reruns—I did when I encountered Jesus in a similar way. "Take me away with You again—pal-ea-se!"

However, the whole point of our time with Him in the natural is not that we should escape *into* Heaven but that we seek to invite the reality of Heaven *here,* into our midst, into the atmosphere of our pain, our mess, our rejection, for incredible miraculous supernatural possibility!

It was God's plan from The Beginning to The End to move in with us. In the spirit and by His Spirit, He does, but not as a mother-in-law would, uninvited, plunking down her suitcases, and barging in white-gloved with a dust mop in tow. More like:

Knock knock.
Who's there?
God.
God who?
The God who loves you.
Oh, God! It's You! (unbolt door). Forgive the mess and *do* come in!
Thank you.
Can you stay, God—forever?
Well that depends...
On what?
Whether you have tea.
Tea?
Eterni-tea...
(Groan).

Angela

◇◇◇◇◇◇◇◇◇◇

And there we are at the kitchen table again with God Almighty—sipping tea throughout eternity. I like the images in the book that keep bringing us back to a home-sweet-home environment. That's where Jesus is the most real to me. While tending to my houseplants, dusting our stuff, knitting a blanket for grandbaby #7, sitting at my computer working, brushing Maggie Doodle Dog, and, of course, working outside in the flower beds, He is always with me.

Although our Lord presents Himself uniquely to each of His children, the constant that binds us all together is the absolute love He has for us. Mack's lack of pain and his garment of "light and color," the display of wildlife, and the beautiful gathering of children were all a picturesque revelation of the Heaven that awaits us. Come Lord Jesus, come!

As we bow our heads in thanks, praise, honor, and glory to the One who is above all others, may we always remember that He is only a breath and blink away. As Donna mentioned near-death experiences, I thought about how full of mystery and excitement they are—the light at the end of the tunnel; the urge to stay in Heaven; the feeling of ultimate love and acceptance. Come Lord Jesus, come!

Tammy

◇◇◇◇◇◇◇◇◇◇

Wow, pass the Puffs—I definitely needed a tissue for Mack's reconciliation with his father. What a tearfully sweet reunion for them, free from the corruptions of the fallen world, finally able to just express their hearts and hurts to one another and find healing. The sniffles start up again just thinking about it.

One thing that struck me as uniquely wonderful in this chapter of celebration, of Heaven coming to earth, was the openness created by the visible rainbows of emotion. Can you imagine a life where all your feelings were plainly visible to those around you, and where there was no means or need to hide them anymore? It seems to me like Heaven will be a place of such pure vulnerability and freedom, the likes of which we'll never know on earth. Yet in Heaven, all our hearts will be open to God and to one another in a place of perfect peace and love and acceptance.

I think Jesus is as excited to have us there as we are to go.

Your Reflections

_____

_____

_____

_____

_____

_____

_____

_____

_____

_____

_____

_____

_____

_____

_____

_____

_____

REFLECTIONS ON *THE SHACK*

_____

_____

_____

_____

_____

_____

_____

_____

_____

_____

_____

_____

_____

_____

_____

_____

16

THE GIFT

Tammy

◇◇◇◇◇◇◇◇◇

For me, reading about Mack's hike with Papa produced the same sense of anticipation as earlier chapters did. The implements, the gift from Sarayu, Papa's quiet manner—and did I mention the chapter title?!—all pointed to a weighty moment in the wilderness. I found myself moving ahead of the narrative in my mind, wondering *How? When? Where? How will Mack be affected? Will I need more tissues nearby?*

Being easy to tears (especially the joyful kind), I was surprised when only a few fell onto the lenses of my reading glasses. The story, as it has done all along, engaged me thoroughly. It remains a cinematic experience in the sense that I can *see* it; I allow myself to be immersed in it. I buy into the characters. I *feel for* Mack. I was relieved that he was not alone. I was glad that he was with the fatherly Papa rather than the "other" Papa. (Papa was right, Mack was going to need his dad at his side for this journey.)

When Papa told Mack that He could have "prevented what happened to Missy," the absence of Mack's rage was conspicuous. He really was being healed; he really had begun to forgive the Father for not intervening on Missy's behalf. He was moving closer to the place where the only anger he harbored was what Papa considered to be appropriate anger.

Forgiving Missy's murderer was not going to be easy, but Mack was ready to take the plunge.

Angela
◇◇◇◇◇◇◇◇◇◇◇

What a powerful chapter! From confusion to costly freedom to reconciliation to revenge to redemption to love and hate to forgiveness and finally to closure, Mack's journey toward total healing was coming full circle. Getting beyond the pain and anger is something that only God can help us do. It is not humanly possible for people to "forgive and forget" when that thorn in our paw keeps the hurt so fresh.

Having Mack deal with the horrible loss of his innocent young daughter puts our losses in perspective. Not that losing your job or dealing with divorce isn't as traumatic for those reeling from it, but the very nature of what Mack was trying to cope with gives the rest of us a hopeful view of the future. After all, if Mack could forgive a murderer with the help of his heavenly Father, surely we can forgive that coworker who drives us crazy, the spouse who snores, the sister who holds grudges, the friend who calls after you're already asleep, the neighbor who leaves his wheelbarrow in his front yard for *four months* (oh, um, sorry for getting carried away).

My point: I'm glad to have read this book (theological differences aside) because of the fundamental truth presented about God's loving and forgiving nature. Allowing God the Father, God the Son, and God the Holy Spirit to shine Light into the unforgiving and judgmental darkness of our humanity brings true freedom and peace of mind, spirit, and soul.

Tammy

◇◇◇◇◇◇◇◇◇◇

Mack certainly needed a Father for this, and of course, Papa knew that very well. He was every bit the perfectly loving Father Mack had always longed to have an open relationship with, and He was there for Mack on this toughest final stretch of a very long hike to healing.

Personally, I'm grateful that it's OK to still be angry, even after forgiving, and that it doesn't make your forgiveness a failure if you have to repeat it a couple kazillion times. I know a lot of people probably feel like Mack did at first—that once you forgive, everything should be fine and dandy again. Papa's explanation is a good dose of truth against this lie that can have people running in circles, wondering what they are doing wrong, just hoping that their forgiveness somehow sticks this time.

In reality, when someone hurts you it's not a one-time thing that you immediately forget. Hurts come back again and again, and every time they do, you either have to choose to cling to that pain, hurting yourself more in the process, or to release it to God and forgive. And then be ready to face the same choice the next time the hurt crops up.

It seems harder than getting crab grass out of a garden bed, but with Papa's grace, we can forgive one another and stop holding grudges that only hurt us.

Shae
◇◇◇◇◇◇◇◇◇◇◇

Ho! Plump with heartrending moments...the chapter starts with A.W. Tozer's wisdom; how that God gives all of Himself *fully* to each one of us. What hope—the knowledge that we are each the apple of His eye—God has billions of favorites to whom He gives love to the power of infinity (Love∞)! Infinity isn't even a number or quantifiable!

God gave Love∞ to little Missy during her ordeal as though there were no other—as He has to Mack, He has to me and billions of people supernaturally at the same time—never diluting His love, presence, or power one measure, oh! Embracing this knowledge empowers us to forgive another and as Tammy said, "by His grace" loose the crabs or whatever from the flower beds and dislodge unforgiveness footholds.

Love came to a young Dutch Jewish woman living in horrifying immoral conditions in the transit camp of Westerbork, the last stop before...Auschwitz. As days turned into weeks turned into months and into two years, Etty Hillesum would drop to her knees and talk to God with regularity, and their hearts fused. Though she knew what lay before her, and despite suffering and injustice, life grew in meaning and beauty as she walked in love with God. Etty knew the rapture of being alive in God's love. Love∞ never left her side. Lying in her barrack thirsty, weak, and with fever, she concluded at the end of her life, "Yet I am also with the jasmine and the piece of sky beyond my window." 1

And yet, so is Mack.
And yet, so am I.

Endnote:

1. *Etty: The Letters and Diaries of Etty Hillesum,* 1941-1943, edited by Klaas A.D. Smelik, translated by Arnold J. Pomerans (Ottawa: Novalis, 2002).

Your Reflections

_____

_____

_____

_____

_____

_____

_____

_____

_____

_____

_____

_____

_____

_____

_____

_____

_____

_____

17

A SPECIAL BOX

Angela

◇◇◇◇◇◇◇◇◇◇

As I read the next chapter, my heart and head was still spinning from the news that our daughter and son-in-law's new #4 baby was not to be. As Mack was inspecting the special box for his Missy, I was coming to terms with a grandchild who would be eternally with the Father. Only God can get people through the pain that this life holds. Only God has the answers to questions that baffle us. Only God.

When sorrows puncture our hearts, will we stay in the warm embrace of our heavenly Father, or do we shut Him out and turn to worldly comforts or well-meaning others? Sometimes only God can kiss the booboo and make it better. Only God can make life worth living again. Only God.

Mack had a decision to make—stay with Papa or return home. He chose to return after he realized that his life mattered. Sharing the bread and wine with his loving and gracious hosts was a fitting farewell. Jesus shed His blood so we can have abundant, joyful life.

I realize every day that I needn't live in an old ugly shack because Jesus has prepared a mansion for me—for each and every one of us—where we will be forever in His presence full of love. That's where our grandbaby is, and I'll be so happy to meet that little one someday.

Donna

We (or should I say "I"?) wake up each morning with an idea of what the day holds. There's a checklist (mental or otherwise). The flight plan (filed with the Tower of Good Intentions). A final systems check (Yes, the espresso machine *is* turned off). A perfect start.

Yet, we never know what the day holds...not *really*. When Mack saw Missy coloring at the table that last time, he didn't *know* it was the last time. Dear Angela, when your daughter announced her pregnancy, you could not see (mercifully!) that your head would be spinning today over the loss of your grandbaby. My heart breaks for you. And yet...

I know that you are possessed of the same hope Mack was. The most brutal circumstances ripped his heart out of his chest. But it continued to beat, however faintly, until a certain day came when he was able to bury Missy's broken body—the emblem of his heartbreak—while bearing a greater awareness of God's love than of his own loss.

Amazing God! He holds our fraying pieces together and re-weaves the seams all at the same time. When we imagine ourselves torn asunder from stem to stern, He comes alongside and holds the barely beating, displaced heart in His hands, guarding it until that certain day comes...a day we expected would be as awful as the one before.

But it's not! The flight plan changed! There was no way of knowing how good it would be. Not *really*.

Shae

◇◇◇◇◇◇◇◇◇◇

I am so sorry for your loss Angela and also honor you for drawing from God's fullness in your pain: beauty for ashes, oil of joy for mourning, jasmine and blue sky for tomorrow, and brilliant flowers for tears just as we see Mack's precious tears bloom in rich soil.

Pssst. Lock this in the vault. Before I actually knew God in relationship, I lacked conviction that He actually considered me important enough to prioritize my needs. This perceived rejection added weight to my anguish, especially when I cried out to Him for Footprint-In-The-Sand-Time. "Pick me up God—help me through this..." Ouch Chihuahua—*violin music please....* Oh, sure, I was on His cosmic "To Do" list but low priority on a long, long scroll:

Item #105: Catch sparrow, return to nest.

Item #1,000,000,000,000,001: Check in on What's-Her-Name.

Slap me silly, one day I finally got it and opened my heart to Him *ahead* of my needs. Consequently, through the intimacy of personal revelation and a progressive unveiling of Jesus in my life, as Mack has experienced, I learned just how often He *had* carried me. Trusting God as Mack now does, I gained confidence to *walk with* Him into my destiny and through my troubles without nearly the need for carrying. Relationship with God and the knowledge and freedom found in His love empowered me to plant my feet with His and move forward—and Mack too will be leaving two sets of footprints in his wake.

Tammy
◇◇◇◇◇◇◇◇◇◇

Reality. It's the end of Mack's weekend at the shack, but it's no fairytale. Spending a weekend with the Trinity has brought Mack a long way, but it has not been a quick fix for everything, and Mack isn't skipping back to Willie's Jeep all hunky-dory. Even with new forgiveness, love, and grace alive in his heart, Mack still feels the pain of Missy's absence, and probably always will. A lost child is never forgotten; Angela, you can probably attest to that quite well right now.

Still, Jesus is there with a hug that lasts as long as you need it, and Papa is taking care of everything. It's not a pat, easy answer that solves everything from here on out, but it's a promise that He'll be there to be your Answer all along the way. It's not simple, like we often want life to be, but it's a very real and true-to-life conclusion to this story.

There are no good-byes. God is still with Mack every bit as much as at the shack, and He's working everything for good, according to His good nature.

Your Reflections

_____

_____

_____

_____

_____

_____

_____

_____

_____

_____

_____

_____

_____

_____

_____

_____

_____

_____

_____

_____

A Special Box

_____

_____

_____

_____

_____

_____

_____

_____

_____

_____

_____

_____

_____

_____

_____

_____

18

FROM HERE OR THERE?

Donna

◇◇◇◇◇◇◇◇◇◇

Now what? That was my initial thought when Mack was t-boned at the end of the last chapter. It was quickly followed by: *Oh no! Don't tell me this book ends with a cliff-hanger. That would be insufferable!*

After all the twists and turns in Mack's story (which made for good reading, BTW), I could not begin to imagine where this "finale" was headed. Correction—I did imagine one thing: that Mack would survive. Or stated more accurately, *I couldn't* imagine that he would die without delivering God's message to Kate.

So, unless this narrative was going to devolve into ghost-story weirdness (perish the thought!), Mack was going to have to pull through. Not only that, but he needed to drag his memory with him. Without it, both he and Kate and the rest of the family, for that matter, could remain stuck in the same awful position they were in before Mack's weekend at the shack—under the crushing weight of *The Great Sadness.*

Thankfully, "the penny dropped and the disjointed story began to crystallize in Mack's mind." Eureka! We don't have to wait for a sequel! Better still, Mack gets to lead Kate to healing, return to his family, and live the rest of his days wrapped, not in "bleak folds of despair," but in the warm embrace of the Father who loves him...

And us.

Shae

Well, I'd also like to see him return to the warm embrace of the brethren, Donna! Drop a pebble in a pond...here we see the amazing ripple effect of Mack's healing time with God flowing through him to Kate as he pulls his daughter free from her quagmire of self-blame and guilt. I pray this ripple effect also heals Mack's relationship with his spiritual family—the Body of Christ, which he left behind with some prejudice and trails of hurt. Perhaps now that he has forgiven God and his earthly father, and has encouraged Kate to forgive herself, he can find it in his heart to reconcile with and forgive his spiritual brothers and sisters for their shortfalls, because the road ahead is a long one to hoe as a Lone Ranger.

While it is sad that the Church failed Mack—that he had to find solace and resolution, Divine relationship and forgiveness in a place of isolation—Mack should be ready now to become a part of a local body of believers. After all, he has just spent the weekend witnessing the power of relationship. As imperfect as we all are—and trust me, my biggest hurts have come from the brethren—the purpose is to belong to each other in devoted relationship just as God the Father is devoted to us, just as Papa, Jesus, and Sarayu are devoted to each other, just as Mack himself is devoted to Nan and his children, just as I am devoted to you, my Powder Room sisters.

If there is a sequel to *The Shack,* I hope it is with a prolonged visit to The Church On The Hill. Hi Yo Silver, Awa-a-ay! (Who *was* that masked blonde?)

Angela

All of a sudden I was back in my 20s when our daughters were young and I was a stay-at-home mom for a few years, and I was watching one of my favorite daytime soaps. Just when the handsome but mysterious nightclub singer was about to ask the beautiful and classy debutante to marry him, she woke up from a dream. Ugh! Then it was another six months to find out it really wasn't a dream—she was actually in a skiing accident and there was never any singer. Ditto ugh!

As Mack tried to sort out what happened to him, when it happened, and possibly why it happened, so it is with us. The harder we try to make sense of nonsense, the more we must depend on Someone greater than ourselves, put our trust into Someone more worthy than anyone else, and place our lives into the hands that hold the universe.

Red marks led the searchers through the woods and over the rocks to Missy—to the place where she was brutally slain. Red marks led His followers to the place where He was crucified upon a tree. His shed blood along the way confirmed that He would be brutally slain—an Innocent not unlike little Missy.

Yet He forgives.

Tammy

◇◇◇◇◇◇◇◇◇◇

I have to say, in this chapter I really identified with Willie. Just watch his reaction to Papa's words, "I am especially fond of you." It's a lot like my reaction the first time I got a personal message straight from God.

I think too many people suffer from the lie that I once believed—that God doesn't speak directly to people anymore. I always sort of figured that the best I could hope for was to read some Scripture verse written to somebody else long ago and maybe it would speak to me...but really, how could I know if I was hearing from God or just reading into things the way I wanted to?

It's sad, but I think I'm far from the only one who ever felt that way. There are a lot of people out there who, like Willie and like me, would really be blown away by the idea that God would bother to send a personal message especially for them...even just a simple one.

Let's do everything we can to bring His words to each one.

Your Reflections

_____

_____

_____

_____

_____

_____

_____

_____

_____

_____

_____

_____

_____

_____

_____

_____

_____

From Here or There?

_____

_____

_____

_____

_____

_____

_____

_____

_____

_____

_____

_____

_____

_____

_____

_____

REFLECTIONS ON *THE SHACK*

19

PERSPECTIVE

Donna

◇◇◇◇◇◇◇◇◇◇

Willie wondered "how to end a tale like this?" The book has a back cover, so we know he found a way. Yet, for me, this is not a story from which you simply walk away and say, "The End." This book turns a switch that can't be shut off after the last page is read.

You could say it sparks imagination, but I think it goes deeper than that. I feel as though this book sparks the recognition of a "knowing" that has been built into the heart of every human being. It's the knowledge, whether expressed or buried under layers of intellectual dissuasion, that—truly—we are *never alone*. Not only are we not alone, but we are in this life with Someone who knows us better than we know ourselves. Someone big enough...strong enough...loving enough...and generous enough to meet us precisely where we are, no matter where "where" is.

Yes, I take issue with certain theological "suggestions" the author of *The Shack* seems to make. And, yes, I urge circumspection (under the guidance of the Holy Spirit) in regard to those "suggestions." Yet, I tip my hat to Wm. Paul Young: He has opened a meaningful dialogue on the sure love of God and created a platform from which we can peer outside our religious "boxes" and see (perhaps with a fresh pair of eyes and a softened heart) that we were created to *literally* walk and talk with Him.

That is quite an accomplishment.

Angela

◇◇◇◇◇◇◇◇◇◇◇

So we've come to the end of another thought-provoking book. How fun it was to explore ideas and ideals with others of differing views and "religious" backgrounds. This book made an impression on me at various levels. As a Christian, I loved the very real and personal interaction Mack had with those at the shack. As a mother, I'm still very disturbed about the whole what-happened-to-Missy scenario. As a sometimes vengeful human being, I was glad that the killer was caught and hope that justice will be served. As a forgiven child of a holy God, I am now a less vengeful person who will strive to live a life worthy of a "good and faithful servant."

No matter the book, there are bytes that stay with you. From *The Shack* there are several that will accompany me along life's journey; but they are only as precious as the thoughts shared by the other writers who are now not only blogger friends but also compatriots in His Kingdom come on earth as it is in Heaven.

Only God can bring together four people who have never met to compose a book full of truisms that resound with people of all ages, races, and senses of humor.

Thanks for journeying with us!

Tammy

◇◇◇◇◇◇◇◇◇◇

I wanted to know what all the hype was about this book—why would so many people be claiming that it changed their lives, while others reviled it as heresy? Turns out that the simple truth of God's love and desire for loving relationship often has both effects. Some didn't know it could be that simple and true and wonderful, and some want to cling to their religious add-ons and rituals.

Whenever I want to find out if there's truth in something regardless of my biases as a human, I'll usually turn to the principle of looking at the fruit. Jesus said that we can recognize the good and bad by what they produce (see Matt. 7:16-18). By that token, if I see lives changed even a little bit the way Willie describes Mack's, well...that's pretty good fruit.

For me, this book has been some amazing fertilizer on the garden of my soul. Sarayu is going to bring forth some good fruit from this, I can tell. ^_^

Shae

◇◇◇◇◇◇◇◇◇◇

The transformation of tragedy through the Father's love spoke voluminously to me in *The Shack*. I commend the book for challenging us to encounter the Living God in relationship. Though we may not see God physically as Mack did, our quest is to love and believe in whom we have not seen, and trust that His tangible presence is possible, even to be anticipated in our lives.

Forgive me if in parts I may have appeared pharisaical in my straining of the odd gnat but note I did not swallow the whole camel. Why would I want to split the timber in two and totally crucify a work that encourages us to seek God? The grand gesture of the message "God is Good" is there.

As Mack learned, Jesus can do more for a grieving soul than any person can. Christ holds in His lap our sorrows. He comes in peace and breathes into us a humble spirit so that we can look up from our empty cradles and say, "It is well with my soul. God is good all of the time." When God began His work of lifting Mack out of his miserable wreck, it did not take Him long to lift it. When Mack stood on the precipice of a grave deep enough to bury him, the sigh of Love pulled him from the edge.

It won't surprise me if some readers of *The Shack* hear a knocking by the Hand of the One who says, "Let Me come in; I will help, comfort, and deliver you." If that happens, I would encourage the person to dust off his or her Bible and ask God through His Word to reveal Who He is, and to discover firsthand why he or she is the object of His special fondness. That personal revelation transformed my own life.

Your Reflections

_____

_____

_____

_____

_____

_____

_____

_____

_____

_____

_____

_____

_____

_____

_____

_____

_____

_____

_____

_____

_____

Perspective

REFLECTIONS ON *THE SHACK*

_____

_____

_____

_____

_____

_____

_____

_____

_____

_____

_____

_____

_____

_____

_____

_____

_____

_____

EPILOGUE

While we were in the Powder Room writing these blogs about this spirit, soul, and mind-boggling book, a neighbor stopped by the house one day for a kitchen-table chat. She asked me if I ever read *The Shack,* and said that she had recently read it and some of what was written resounded deeply. But she also thought it put God in yet another man-made box—this time a "politically correct" one.

Why is it so hard for us to just let God be God, an omnip-otent, omniscient God who just IS, and IS the great I AM without human limitations? I suppose because He is too big and too wonderful for our finite minds to comprehend such a loving and merciful One in Three. After all even Adam and Eve who walked with Him in the most beautiful garden ever created had trouble accepting all that He was. "There must be something more…"

We may find out just how small our minds and world really are when we plunge into the third book in our Powder Room series: Reflections from the Powder Room on *90 Minutes in Heaven* by Don Piper.

You are very welcome to join us again as we hop, skip, and stumble through sorting out this thing called life with as much finesse as our stilettos (or pink bunny slippers) allow, with as much seriousness as we can muster while keeping stiff upper ruby-red lips, and as much joy as we can share while sitting before the mirror of our souls.

OUR STORIES

Shae

It was a dark and stormy night...

No, really! Please indulge my use of this dramatic opening cliché because it best describes the state of my heart on the evening that I found myself a "suddenly single" mother. Afraid, alone, and at odds with God, whom I felt should have intervened long before I had to become a human shield to deflect words and actions that pierced and hurt so deeply; my heart really was in torment. Where was God when we needed Him, when darkness pervaded my home? Where was the God of "Call and I will answer thee?" I'd held out a Lois Lane-ish hope that Superman would catch me sometime before I went *splat;* that it was only a matter of time before He emerged from a cosmic telephone booth for a spectacular God-is-faithful-God-is-true three-feet-from-the-ground save.

So when my life did go *splat,* for all intent, I really did wonder, and wrestled with whether He even cared about me...us. I needed Him even more now to help bring light to our present end. Would He, and faster than a speeding bullet?

After I soothed my son to sleep on the makeshift emergency mattress my neighbor had placed on the floor, I took my turn to weep. Rejection was something I had to deal with; fear, and this distance I felt from God. From the sewer of misery, my heart waxed anguish. I was afraid to call out to the Lord because if He did not answer me, my heart would surely turn to stone. On the other hand, He was our hope, so I grabbed my Bible, which I was grateful to have. Miraculously, my eight-year-old had reminded me that we needed it in addition to my purse and Mr. Bear, the only three things we toted down the street in haste with us. Bless his wise heart; he saw my Bible as *my* security blanket.

In the absence of words I could not muster, I clasped the Good Book, sandwiching it between my son, Mr. Bear, and me, hoping God would somehow read our hearts and give us some sign that He was in control and present. Mercifully, I fell asleep—my last thought, that I didn't know how I could ever arise and face the things that lay ahead alone, without assurance of God's love and intervention.

Enter a man into my dreams that night whom I knew to be Jesus because His eyes were gentle and beautiful, His voice soft and velvety, and His countenance compassionate and patient. Jesus was everything opposite of what I had known to be true of man—gentle, soft-spoken, intense, with eyes that burned passion. Of course my heart pounded and I fell in love instantly, especially when He grasped my hands and drew them to His breast. "I love you, and I want to take care of you both."

He showed us a huge house on a hill and led us into fragrant rooms filled with everything we needed, the things we longed for. Everything seemed strangely déjà vu, familiar. He told me this was one of many mansions in His Father's house—and it represented our hearts, a beautiful place He dwelt in with us, a place He would never leave, and a place where we could always find Him if we search for Him first above anything else.

I awoke and He was gone. "Jesus, Jesus, Jesus," I cried with longing, desiring to see His face again but ultimately satisfied that I had; content that Love had filled my heart's emptiness, that we were not alone. God led me to Himself even when my heart was too overwhelmed to ask. That place met the root of our deepest desires, filled the gap of a lost relationship, and caught us into His arms in flight.

Just as Mack, Nan, and the children had to begin life anew minus a loved one, my son and I have started over—buttercups and dandelions on new windowsills, Mr. Bear and my Bible close by, and with God very much dwelling with us. Truth be told, He never left. Though our prayers may still begin with tears, they end with praise. Pain that ultimately leads us to God *always* becomes a good thing.

Donna

◇◇◇◇◇◇◇◇◇◇◇

Twenty years ago, I experienced a devastating betrayal. Bards and balladeers from Shakespeare to The Supremes have immortalized similar tales of woe. I needn't bore you with the gory details; the word *betrayal* speaks for itself.

Something was wrong, yet everyone including me remained silent, refusing to believe the unbelievable. Surely our suspicions were unfounded; certainly our imaginations had run amok. I remember asking myself, *How can you suspect such things of this good friend? What is wrong with you, anyway?*

There came a day, however, when I realized that the Holy Spirit had been revealing the unsavory truth to my heart, for my protection and for the preservation of the offender. I decided to confront the issue head-on; I invited my friend to lunch and asked the inevitable point-blank question. The answer? A brick wall of denial.

In the ensuing weeks, it became clear that the only thing left to do was to move on. In time I relocated, but the weight of the betrayal traveled with me. It was lodged in my chest, alternately transmitting waves of searing heat and numbing cold through the hollowed chambers of my heart. Its weight was crushing; I could barely breathe.

A couple of months later, a friend from our circle called to say she was praying for me. She, too, had known something sinister was going on; like me she'd doubted herself. Meanwhile, the destruction had spread rapidly. What I experienced was nothing compared to what others were enduring.

That phone call was God's doing, a single, powerful ray of light shed in a very dark place. Still, it would be months before my healing was complete. Then one unexpected night, God revealed the way of escape: it was unconditional forgiveness. I protested: "Forgiveness? I've already forgiven her!" That is when He showed me the rotting bodies buried deep in my soul: anger and outrage...rejection and fear...judgment and self-pity. Mercifully, He showed me how to turn the whole putrid mess over to Him, and in an instant the long winter of my soul turned to spring. It was like being born again— again! My life went from black and white to living color. Everything seemed fresh and new. I wanted the friend who'd hurt me to experience the same freedom. I wanted to talk to her, but she was nowhere to be found.

Then, out of the blue, she called—more than 12 years later! The debacle had taken a toll on her; she couldn't go another day without making things right. She asked my forgiveness. I explained that I'd forgiven her long ago. Still, she needed to hear it. For me the sting was long gone—but her night of freedom had just arrived.

That experience gave me so much. I learned to trust the leading of the Holy Spirit. I learned the importance of confronting issues head-on. I learned that healing is always available. Most of all, I learned that forgiveness is freedom.

Angela
◇◇◇◇◇◇◇◇◇◇◇◇

No Doubts

The Shack was full of doubting. Mack doubted the authenticity of the note in the mailbox. Willie doubted his friend's motives. Kate doubted her innocence in her sister's death. Nan doubted Mack's story. Mack doubted the reality of his shack experience.

As I thought about doubts we all have at times, I thought of Mrs. Sester Rideout and how she never for a moment doubted her heavenly Father.

For as far back as I can remember Mrs. Rideout (we called each other Mrs. out of true respect for one another) was one of only six African Americans who lived in our small town nestled in the Cumberland Valley in southcentral Pennsylvania. She and her husband raised their family and then they raised their grandchildren "with the help of my heavenly Father," she would say after almost every sentence.

After her husband passed away she started attending our church that was within walking distance of her small house—a home overflowing with love, sentimental treasures, and family photos.

Full of "frozen chosen" Presbyterians, Mrs. Rideout's spontaneous praising of the Lord with raised hands and out-loud "amens" raised more than one stoic's eyebrow over the years.

But her genuine love of God and others caused even the most stiff-necked to soften. Or so I thought.

Our friendship spanned 20 some years and one time while visiting Mrs. Rideout, I told her how much I admired her honest and sincere worship and praise of God in such a quiet and non-emotional environment. Although we were alone in her home, she leaned toward me and in a small voice said, "One day after church a man came over to me and said, 'Sester, we don't speak out or raise our hands here in this church during service.' And, Mrs. Shears, do you know what I told him? I said, 'Sir, when I'm praisin' my Lord and Savior, I don't see no Presbyterians!'"

Hallelujah! Mrs. Rideout was a true believer. Her God came first; He was the One she wanted to please. She knew a personal God who was her Deliverer and her Best Friend. Mrs. Rideout went to be with the Lord a few years ago when she was in her 90s. The "going home" service was held in our church, and as the gospel choir cried out celebrations of a life well lived and pastors from her previous churches shouted their love of her and God, tears of joy ran down my face as I realized how Mrs. Rideout was witnessing to us even still.

I praise God for this dear saint's life. She left a permanent mark on the hearts of many people—especially mine.

Tammy

◇◇◇◇◇◇◇◇◇◇◇

In His Arms

In the end, Mack had to leave the shack, but God went with him. God is always there.

I'm deeply grateful for God's presence with each individual—my heart couldn't rest over certain people unless I knew they were held in the Father's arms. I am reminded of a student I had once in a tenth grade English class.

It was in a poor school in a very blue-collar area. Most of the students were extremely unmotivated, came from broken families in low socioeconomic backgrounds, and enjoyed very few opportunities. I was only there for two months before my prearranged departure, so I truly did not expect to create any kind of revolution in my classroom. I just prayed that I could make some little difference in a few young lives while I was there.

In one of my classes there was a boy—we'll call him Jimmy. Jimmy was one of the students (and there were a few) who had not learned much about hygiene...by tenth grade. He was ill-kept and very ill-mannered; after only a few days observing, I realized that the class as a whole would be much easier to manage when Jimmy decided to put his head down and sleep. He did this about four days out of five, and when he wasn't sleeping through class he was a constant disruption.

He had several learning disabilities, but was held back more by his strong anti-motivation. He seemed to actually be *trying* to fail.

For almost two months, I was going to be teaching writing to Jimmy's class. I didn't even know if I could expect Jimmy to *do* the writing assignments. And of course, I had 25 other students just in that one class to worry about.

I did the only thing I could do—presented Jimmy to the Lord in prayer and asked Him to help me help this boy in any way I could. And you know, Jesus was all over it.

Jimmy's home life was bad. Very, very bad. In fact, shortly before I came, he had moved in with his grandmother because his mother (the only parent even in the picture) was in jail. I never met Jimmy's grandmother, but I did hear of her impact—she wouldn't stand for Jimmy failing English. It was a minor push, but the need to bring his grade up made Jimmy at least start trying.

He also took a little interest in what we were doing. I was teaching writing through creative writing, which was a change for all the students. Jimmy's writing was a huge struggle for him, and I won't say he improved by leaps and bounds either. He was, by the end, still writing below an average fourth grader's level.

I encouraged him where I could. I made allowances for his learning disabilities where I could. I also had incorporated how well the students worked in class into the grade, and was happily able to give Jimmy good scores in that area. He worked very slowly and was sometimes very frustrated, but he was working in class, making a consistent effort, and I was happy to see it. I spent as much time as I could spare in helping him, guiding his understanding. I was also able to encourage one of his classmates to help him; I even saw him come to me outside of class for help.

Jimmy turned in every writing assignment. They weren't "A" papers, but they still helped. By the end of my time there, I was able to give Jimmy his progress report and congratulate him on having a passing grade in English.

It was one of those bittersweet experiences as a teacher—I had seen a student improve, yet I knew he needed so much more, and I was powerless to help him. My hands were tied by my position in many ways. Just before I left, I heard that his mother was being released, and he was going to be taken away from his grandmother again. Then and now, all I can do about that is pray. I can only turn this boy over to the Lord, and trust his love for Jimmy to "prosper him, and not to harm him," and "to give him hope and a future."

In the end, I had to leave that school, but God stayed with Jimmy. God will always stay with him.

Glossary

blister-bakers–virtual, foot-torturing shoes worn by those who insist upon walking around the same old mountain *again*

btw–the texter's thumb-saving way to say "by the way"

bytes–small digestible phrases that sink into your psyche; can be long- or short-term

compatriots–people of the same country, or citizens of God's Kingdom

crab grass–a gardener's most loathed nemesis

daytime soap operas–some afternoon TV shows full of over-dramatized characters, scenes, and situations that serve as distractions from your own life full of overdramatized characters, scenes, and situations

duh–affirmative answer to the question, "Was it that obvious?"

ditto ugh!–see "Ugh!" then times 2

eating the meat and spitting out the bones–chewing well on what you hear and only swallowing truth (you are what you "eat")

fresh pair of eyes–opposite of droopy, mascara-laden, contact-tired eyes

frozen chosen–tongue-in-cheek stereotype expression about Presbyterians; proven true in some cases

Hmmm...–a thoughtful pause

hunky-dory–ain't got no worries

IMHO–In my humble opinion

ka-ching!–We're in the money...dead on...perfecto mondo!

kazillion–a seemingly limitless quantity; standard measure for counting number of shoes owned by most women

lap-band surgery–laproscopic gastric band surgery, a literal squeeze on the appetite

Love–"shaeism" for love to the power of infinity; snowman laying on its side *is* the mathematical symbol for infinity. No. Really.

Maggie–short for Margaret Thatcher; happiest Old English Sheepdog on the planet

OMG–Oh My Gosh!

Ouch Chihuahua–Excited utterance by a Canadian shoe-aholic

Plank-in-Eye-Disease–leads to hoof and mouth disease if not removed

POV: Point of View; Prada or Vuitton?

PR–Public Relations; something God's people need to be good at

Psst–Hey you, I want your attention

red herring–diversionary form of logic akin to throwing spaghetti against the wall and hoping it sticks

religious boxes–what people like to put God in (Note: It doesn't work)

shoot from the hip–tell it like it is, no sugar-coating

slap me silly–a casual remark not to be taken seriously by bystanders meaning, "OMG, if my IQ were any higher, I'd be a vegetable."

truism–a self-evident truth, as in, "Yes, I really do need another pair of loafers."

ugh!–means "What?!" "Are you kidding me?!" "That is *so* lame!" "No way!"

vault–to lock something in the vault means: "Don't you tell a soul, or else!"

word nerd–one who has to try hard not to correct everybody's grammar; or, one whose eyes light up when the preacher starts throwing Greek and Hebrew around

RECOMMENDED READING

A Message From God by Retha and Aldo McPherson

Call Me Crazy, But I'm Hearing God by Kim Clement

Dreams and Visions by Joe Ibojie

His Manifest Presence by Don Nori Sr.

Hope Beyond Reason by Dave Hess

Tales of Brokenness by Don Nori Sr.

The Supernatural Power of a Transformed Mind by Bill Johnson

The Unseen World of the Holy Spirit by Frank Bailey

When Heaven Invades Earth by Bill Johnson